Awake Apprentice

Awake Apprentice

A system for transforming your job into a creative career

by Hilary Jane Grosskopf

Awake Apprentice (Black & White Print Edition)
Copyright © 2020 by Awake Solutions LLC

ISBN: 978-1-7323583-4-8

All rights reserved. No part of this book may be reproduced in any form, except in the context of reviews and fair reference, without written permission from Awake Solutions LLC.

Illustrations by Aaron Bardo, SOL Vision

Contents

Preface   **i**

Introduction   **1**

Chapter 1: Interests   **19**

Chapter 2: Possibility   **49**

Chapter 3: Potential   **91**

Chapter 4: Relativity   **123**

Chapter 5: Synthesis   **163**

Chapter 6: Creativity   **199**

Conclusions   **247**

Appendices   **259**

"It is better to strive in one's own dharma

than to succeed in the dharma of another.

Nothing is ever lost in following one's own dharma,

but competition in another's dharma

breeds fear and insecurity."

The Bhagavad Gita

Translation by Eknath Easwaran

Preface

Preface to Awake Apprentice

What is the right job for me? What is the purpose of my job and my career? How can I tap into my creativity despite the demands of my day-to-day work?

These are some of the questions I asked myself during the early years of my career, just a few years after joining the working world. Though I had the opportunity to work for some amazing organizations, I felt as though something was missing. In some jobs, I suffered from poor leadership and culture. At other jobs, I lacked opportunities to grow personally and professionally. I craved opportunities to be creative but felt uninspired and exhausted from my day-to-day work. When I talked to friends and colleagues, I found that many of them were frustrated with work and career development as well.

It took a lot of personal reflection and introspection to unravel the problem at the root of my uneasiness and unhappiness. I finally realized that my career had unfolded the way it did because I had taken opportunities that didn't quite add up to a meaningful, engaging work experience for me. I was progressing down a safe but inauthentic path that didn't feel sustainable. I craved opportunities to be creative. *What could I do?*

I needed to find a job that aligned with my interests, fulfilled my personal needs, and allowed me to grow personally and professionally. I had to find deeper purpose and exercise my creativity. My story about how I took the leap into a more creative career and lifestyle is the story that I share in this book. It led to the creation of the Awake Apprentice path.

Awake Apprentice is a how-to guide for navigating your career, discovering your purpose, tapping into your unique creative powers, and finding freedom. It is a guide for embracing your work experience in order to create your own original solutions and offerings. This holistic, work-life integration approach gave me the ability to find jobs where I felt more aligned and engaged. I experienced an abundance of personal and professional growth.

As I used the mindset and approach that I share in the book to navigate my job search, the experience of working for someone else turned from painful to constructive, and from limiting to expansive. I turned obstacles into learning opportunities. I found opportunities for developing solutions and adding new value at work. Eventually, I started to develop my own creative contributions. In the Conclusion section, I share more about the powerful, transformative impacts of taking a leap and embracing your creative potential.

Whether you are just starting on your career journey, considering a job or career change, or wondering whether you should start your own venture, this book provides actionable guidance for navigating your career decisions with more awareness and confidence. I hope this guide serves as a roadmap for gathering experiences of applied learning and moving toward your creative potential.

xo Hilary

Introduction

Do your work.

When someone asks you "What do you do for work?", what is your answer? Whether you are a young professional or a seasoned one, your work is probably something that you think about pretty much every day of your life. Consider just how much time and focus you spend on work in a given day (and maybe during the night, too). Ironically, most people seldom pause to ask themselves: *How is my work adding value to my life, the lives of others, and the world?*

You might be thinking, as many people do: Well, obviously, work provides income so that I can live my life. And, who has time to think about how work affects others and the world? However, since you're reading this book, I think you're on a higher playing field, seeing that your work must have more meaning than a paycheck... and it does.

In our modern world, work has become a means to an end for many people. Many people work in order to fund life outside of work. This is largely a result of the **work-life balance approach**. A work-life balance approach encourages us to find a balance between work time and personal time. The word "balance" sounds healthy but it actually encourages a disconnection or a separation between our work and our lives, which is causing a lot of individual and societal suffering. The work-life balance approach has led us to a place in our history where many people are detached from the meaning and impact of their own work. Many are also accustomed to believing that work should be unsatisfying and maybe even painful in order to deserve something preferred or pleasurable in return. This work-life balance approach has led to a rise in depression, wasted time, and wasted effort. Whether we intentionally aim to find work-life balance or not, many people confront the negative impacts of work-life balance every day. It's deeply ingrained in our social patterns and corporate human resources programs.

During my early career, I experienced the negative impacts of a work-life balance approach. I found that these negative results stem from three major issues. You might realize that you have also suffered from one or more of these issues that stem from a work-life balance approach. The first issue is that many of us are **detached from the impacts of our work**. We are unaware of the real impacts of our work on others and the world, and therefore we do not feel connected to the value or purpose. I know this because I experienced it myself and I have seen so many cases of this in the workplace. Maybe you have seen it on your team or experienced it, too. This is a big problem because no matter how detached we become or how good we get at work-life balance, the impacts of our work still exist and persist. Everything is connected.

The second issue is that we **simply don't enjoy doing the work**. The results of work in terms of salary and prestige or praise might be great, but the process of doing the work feels dull or stressful. This is unsustainable and also results in feeling empty and unmotivated, at work and in life. Notice that I wrote that "we simply don't enjoy doing the work" and not just "doing work". This is because even though sometimes we say that it's just work and no one enjoys it, I truly believe (and I have found to be true in my own experience) that certain work is enjoyable for each of us, it just might not be the specific work you're doing right now.

Finally, we often **don't have opportunities to express our own creativity at work**! Creativity is part of every human's DNA and when we do have the opportunity to express our creativity at work, great solutions and creations emerge that release our true potential and help us evolve as a society. The ability to express our creativity also contributes to better mental health and overall well-being.

The work-life balance approach encourages us to "do your work" at work, but it most often does not incorporate opportunities for creativity. The work-life balance approach encourages you to find creative outlets outside of work only, which is actually taking potential away from the individual and the company, too, in terms of innovation.

There is an undeniable connection between work and life, and this is why the work-life balance approach is the wrong way to look at work and the wrong way to build a career. The work you do is such a big part of your life. It can make your life meaningful and enjoyable. It's frustrating that it often seems like work has the opposite effect for so many of us. The good news is that this book provides an alternative to the work woes and disconnection so many of us face. The Awake Apprentice approach is a path for solving all three of these issues and freeing yourself from the work-life balance approach.

Now, let's actually define **work** to underscore why we need a new alternative to the work-life balance approach. When you do a simple online search, there are not many definitions of the word (aside from the physics definition). Here is my definition and the definition we'll use throughout this book: **Work is a specific collection or sequence of actions we take to contribute something of value to another**. Taking the money aspect out of it, work is simply a way that we each channel and give our energy in order to produce something of value. You should be connected with and invested in the impacts of your work in order to see the value. Work does not have to be painful or exhausting. You should be able to express your creativity at work. Why not?

When we zoom out, there is a complex web of issues in the modern working world. There is empty or value-less work that seems to have value. There is valuable work that feels unsatisfying for the people executing the work each day. This book is about zooming in on your own work aspirations and the impacts on yourself, other people, and the world in order to lead by example as part of the solution. A new solution often involves a shift or a transformation in the what or the how of your own approach to work.

The need for a higher level of awareness about your work and a way to feel good about the work you do is the motivation for the Awake Apprentice journey. It is a shift from work-life balance to **work-life integration**. If you're on board for this journey, consider yourself an Awake Apprentice. Get ready to learn how to connect to the impacts of your work, find work that you enjoy, and unleash your ability to express your creativity at work. But first, you need to get a job.

Get a job.

What if I told you that the first step in solving the work-life balance crisis is to… Get a job?! This might be the last thing you want to hear, but according to statistics, you probably already have a job or you're looking for one. No matter how you feel about your job or your search right now, it's actually good news that you're in a position to begin this journey toward greater alignment, creativity, and freedom.

A **job** is a name or descriptor for the work you do. Behind every job title and description is a vivid collection of work-related actions. **A job is a universally understandable term for communicating the type of work you do and the level of expertise you have**. Most of us who are currently employed can state in one, two, or three words what our job is called. I'm an engineer. I'm a doctor. I'm a cashier. I'm a writer. I'm a driver. I'm an artist. I'm a flight attendant. I'm a project manager. There are so many jobs out there that all relate back to work that is needed or "in demand".

Job titles are helpful for job searches. They are very simple, concise words that encompass the specific set of actions that result in value - the work! At work, job titles are helpful for understanding what different people are responsible for within an organization. However, they often cause anxiety and animosity over power and salary. Some jobs titles have a good reputation and others do not. The irony is that some of the most undesirable jobs are the most vital to our society in terms of impact and they are actually enjoyable for the right person! For the purposes of our Awake Apprentice journey, I encourage you to drop your pre-existing biases about certain jobs and job titles. Keep an open mind. With a positive and creative approach, all jobs can be experiences of learning, as well as a means for discovering your true potential.

Ultimately, a job is a vehicle for doing work in the world. Work is an action and therefore a platform for experiencing the world, learning more about ourselves, and connecting with other people. A job is a vehicle for transformation.

This is exactly what I will teach you how to do in this book: To use your job as a means for finding meaningful purpose through impact, enjoying your days, and unleashing your creative potential.

Even though you're working toward work-life integration in this book, your job does not need to be your whole life. We all have many layers and we all need time away from doing our jobs. **The work-life integration approach is about finding a job that is intrinsically motivating, meaningful, and enjoyable.** It's about using your time away from work to fuel your best work, and your time at work to reach your potential and enjoy your life (even when you're at work!).

The final professional term to explore before embarking on the Awake Apprentice path is **career**. Let's look at how your work and your job influence the larger picture: your career path.

Focus on Your Career.

Everyone has very different ways of approaching career planning. For some people, they choose a career very early on and stick with that specific career trajectory. For others, a career is a winding road of jobs that amounts to a unique patchwork blanket of different experiences. For most people, it's somewhere in between.

It's funny how at any specific moment, when we're truly present, our work and our job are easy to define. However, defining our career requires looking at our past work experience or looking ahead at our future work aspirations. **A career is a specific progression of work contributions that leaves a certain impact and value for others**. A career takes a job or singular work experience and turns it into a progression of work contributions that build on each other.

As an Awake Apprentice, it's important to zoom out from time-to-time and think about your career. Why? A career perspective allows you to envision your work experiences on a horizon of life-long value. It's not that you need to plan your whole career and your life out now; we are constantly changing and evolving. However, thinking about your career and your future helps you to think about the impact and direction of your work. Thinking about career is a great way to facilitate a shift to a new job or line of work, if necessary. It also helps when considering how to start your own creative project or your own business venture by harnessing your skills and experience.

I won't tell you whether I believe that a straight-line career trajectory is more valuable or enjoyable than a winding career path or not, because both can serve as vehicles for creativity. There is a different approach for each person. I know from experience that career planning can feel overwhelming and intimidating. Career planning often involves making decisions and committing to an identity far before we're really ready or confident in doing so. This is why I'll encourage you to drop career planning for the purposes of this journey. Instead, think in terms of your **career development** and your **creative vocation development**. For me, this is a much more exciting approach for building a career and seeing it as a journey of professional development and personal growth.

Many talented rising leaders doubt that they have the ability to find work that makes an impact, that is enjoyable to do, and provides creative opportunities. It's easy to fall into auto-pilot mode of checking the boxes on tasks and following a conveyor-belt career path. The Awake Apprentice approach is a system for helping you reflect on your current work and job in order to build a meaningful, satisfying career. By working through this guidebook, I hope you will realize that you can forge your own authentic and interesting career path, despite the enticing comfort and ease of following the norm. Awake Apprentice is a system for finding work-life integration.

Awake Apprentice is about finding freedom by pushing past the norm and discovering your creative potential even in uncomfortable or unconventional places that might force you to go out on your own and share something creative at work, as your own side project, or as your own business venture. I hope that you will feel inspired to lead by example and encourage others to find more freedom and creativity at work as well. Now, let's look at the journey.

◆ ◆ ◆

The Six Phases of the Awake Apprentice Approach

The journey to finding an authentic vocation and reaching your creative potential is a winding path. In this book, I'll guide you through six phases, which are like lenses for viewing and navigating different essential elements of your job search and creative journey. Each of the six phases has its own chapter with insights, stories, and interactive exercises for shaping your approach to work and career development. Here, I'll provide a quick overview of the six phases in the Awake Apprentice journey.

The first phase of the Awake Apprentice journey is **Interests**. Your interests are the foundation of the Awake Apprentice path. Interests are products, services, and experiences that evoke connection, joy, and inspiration. When was the last time you really focused on and identified your true interests? By reconnecting with your interests, you'll learn how to choose jobs that are meaningful, impactful, and enjoyable.

Next, we move on to the second phase, **Possibility**. In the second chapter, you'll learn how to gather the right support for doing your best work. We'll explore the elements of possibility, which include salary, leadership, environment, culture, and

The Awake Apprentice System

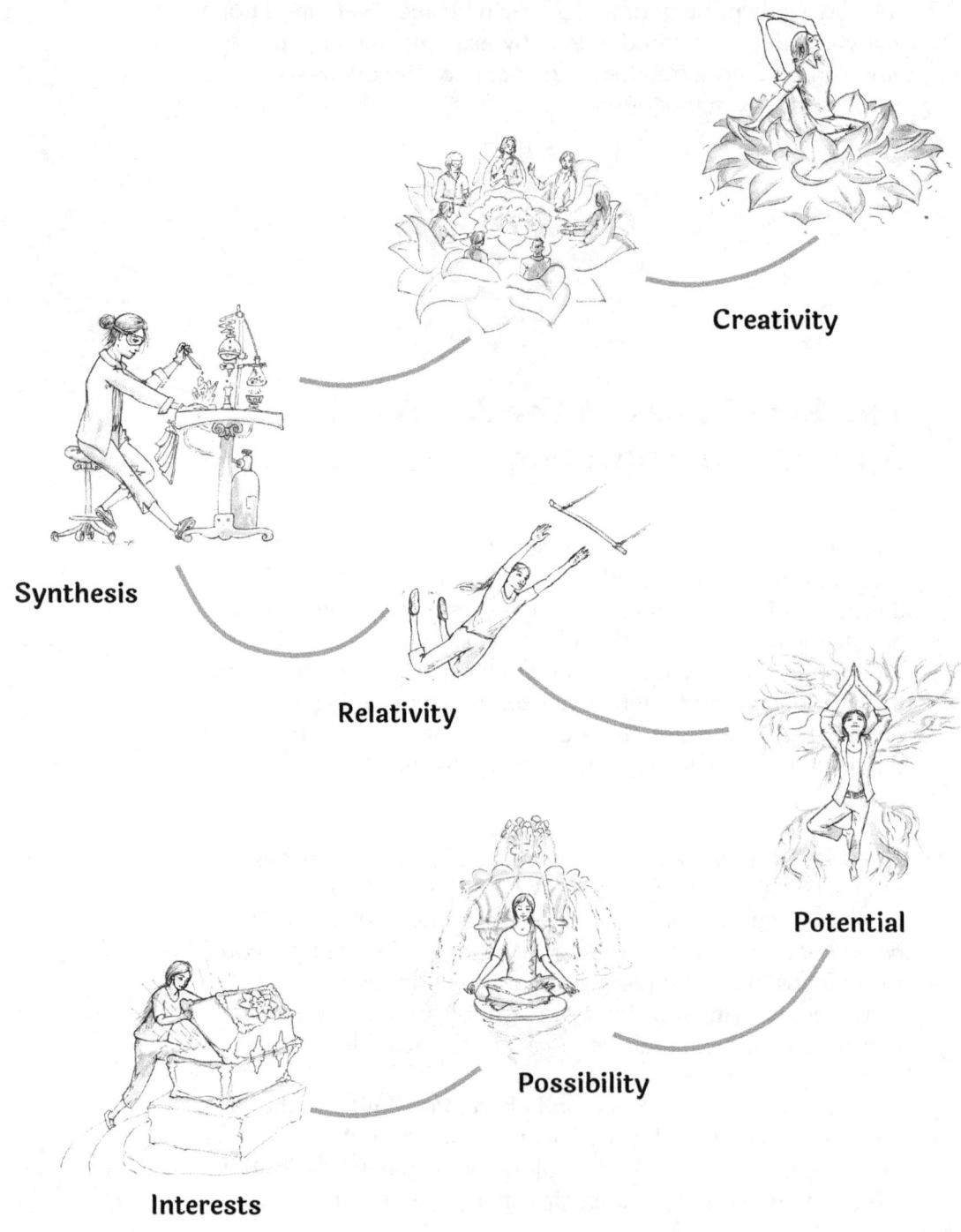

schedule. In order to enjoy the process of working and leading, you need a job with the right support.

After Possibility, we move on to **Potential**. The Potential chapter is all about discovering your potential at work by finding opportunities for learning and development. Potential is at the heart of the Awake Apprentice experience. As someone reading this book, you know that you are motivated to learn. You believe in yourself and your potential. Learning and development are what unleash new potential. Opportunities for learning and development turn a job into an apprenticeship. When you immerse in experiences of applied learning, you build a real-world tool belt for making impactful contributions and seeing your own creative potential as well.

The first three chapters of the Awake Apprentice path form the base for finding a meaningful and enjoyable job and embarking on your creative journey. Chapters 4, 5, and 6 are the steps for transforming your job into a creative career, creative project, or creative venture.

In chapter 4, we embark on the exciting phase of **Relativity**. In this chapter, you'll learn about the importance of gathering a diverse array of experiences that fuel your ideas and understanding. A diverse array of contexts and work experiences spark ideas, original solutions, and creative contributions. Relativity is important for meeting different kinds of people, developing your capabilities, discovering your purpose, and learning different ways to solve real-world problems.

After gathering different types of work experience and perspectives, it's time for **Synthesis**. In chapter 5, you'll learn how to use your unique set of work and life experiences to really awaken your creativity. You'll learn practices for coming up with your own new ideas and solutions!

In the final chapter, **Creativity**, you'll learn how to actually manifest your solutions and creations. The creative process is the vehicle for turning your big ideas into actual products, services, or experiences. The ability to plan and execute is key for creative success.

The last three chapters will likely push you out of your comfort zone, in terms of your mindset and your actions. **I will prompt you to take the lead of your career by finding your authentic purpose and freedom using the wisdom gained from your unique realm of experiences at work and in life.** In doing so, you'll find that you can solve problems and manifest creative contributions that make an impact and provide value for others. Your relationship to work will transform and you'll find new fuel for developing your own creative ideas, project, or vocation.

Although many people think of creativity as artwork or something far out, it doesn't have to be. While your creative contribution might be artsy, many of us have creative potential that is applicable in a business environment or a more structured sense as well. In this book, creativity applies to a wide realm of creative contributions, including new solutions and original works of all kinds. As you progress on the Awake Apprentice path, you'll find your creative niche that speaks to your interests, strengths, and experience.

Also, awakening your creativity doesn't require leaving your job or working for yourself. Some people might find that working creatively and manifesting a creative contribution means starting their own business venture. Others will find that awakening creativity comes into play at work in a large or small organization, as a way to contribute more innovative ideas and work with more freedom.

By working through the Awake Apprentice system, you will be able to choose a job with more confidence and transform your job into a creative career. Whether you are just starting on your career journey or considering a pivot, this system provides the guidance for moving forward with confidence. Finally, before we jump into Chapter 1, let's take a closer look at how to work through the guidebook.

Working through the Guidebook

This guidebook is designed to be an interactive experience. I organized the book so that you can work through each section and immediately apply the guidance in your day-to-day work and life. This approach requires no technology or investment other than your time and attention. I hope it is something you look forward to reading and working through each day as part of your morning routine, your lunch break at work, or your evening wind-down before bed.

✎ The Organization

The guidebook contains six chapters that correspond to the six phases of the Awake Apprentice path. I encourage you to begin with Chapter 1: Interests, and read the book in the order it is presented. The order is important because it follows a natural progression. Missing a phase could mean that you don't achieve the objective of the Awake Apprentice system. Your likelihood of finding a job you love, gathering relevant experiences, and manifesting your own creations is higher if you work through the book in the order the chapters are presented and then go back to take a closer look at the chapters that you find require more of your time and focus. After the six chapters, there is a conclusion with some important next steps, parting guidance, and a closing reflection.

✎ Stories from the Field

In each chapter, in addition to content about that specific phase, I offer a story from my own work experience to illustrate that phase in action. My stories from the field are meant to give you an applied example. However, everyone's experience is completely different. Use the stories as supplementary information and inspiration.

✎ Reflections and Exercises

We learn the most when we apply our learnings and put them into action sooner than later. I encourage you to do the reflection and exercises after reading each chapter. Use the reflections at the end of each chapter and the associated exercises as tools for your progress and as part of your experience of applied learning. By <u>writing</u> down your answers, you'll gain the ability to think more independently and creatively.

The exercises are vehicles for integrating the content from this book into your life in order to begin to take action. You'll see the concepts come to life if you do the reflections and exercises thoroughly. The goal is to put the ideas into action while they're fresh in your mind!

✎ The Pace

The best thing about a book is that you can work through it at your own pace and on your own time. This is great because it offers flexibility. However, it can be challenging for some because it requires discipline. If you are someone who needs a bit of structure and guidance, there is a sample schedule in the back of the book. You can use this to work through the book with consistency and follow through. I suggest working through a chapter every week and really take the time to read, understand, and integrate each phase. Of course, everyone has their own pace and schedule, so spend as much time as you need with each section.

Let's begin!

What will you learn? What will you contribute? What will you create? Let's get started with a short introductory reflection before diving into your interests.

Introductory Reflection

What is the work you do, currently?

_____

_____

_____

_____

Do you enjoy the work you do? Why or why not?

_____

_____

_____

_____

How does your work impact yourself, your team, your organization, and the world?

_____

_____

_____

_____

Introductory Reflection

What would your career progression look like if you stayed in your current industry or field of work?

_____

_____

_____

_____

Does this career progression excite and inspire you? Why or why not?

_____

_____

_____

_____

What is your intention for embarking on the Awake Apprentice journey?

_____

_____

_____

_____

Chapter 1

Interests

Lead with Your Interests

Think back to your early days in school. You probably remember learning about a handful of different jobs. Friends and family chose jobs for different reasons. In a rapidly changing society with many choices and competition for work, it's no wonder that it feels overwhelming to choose the right job. It's also challenging to decide how to pivot in your career when you realize that your current job is not in alignment with your needs or intended impact. There are many aspects of a job that make it sustainable, fulfilling, enjoyable, and impactful. Where should you begin when searching for the perfect job?

What if I told you that the first step in finding the right job is to figure out what you're interested in? This means putting aside thoughts about what you're good at, what others tell you to do, or what you're told is needed or valuable in the marketplace. These factors are important but they should not be the primary considerations when choosing a job. Awake Apprentices first focus on their interests. It might seem crazy, but this is the way to find a truly satisfying job and achieve work-life integration.

Interests are the products, services, and experiences that you find in your treasure chest of life. Just like a pirate loves the thrill of seeking out and finding treasure, Awake Apprentices love following their interests. True interests evoke joy, connection, and inspiration. This first chapter is all about understanding your interests and learning how to lead with your interests when navigating your job search.

When you leave for work in the morning, do you ever feel as though your main goal is to just get through the day? When you identify and understand your interests, you will be able to find work that is motivating and inspiring. With this genuine motivation, you will get up each day excited to go to work. You will find a natural sense of dedication and take ownership with ease. You'll feel more aligned in your actions and impacts at work. Work will feel like an experience of applied learning, where you get to learn more about your interests.

Interests are the products, services, and experiences that you find in your treasure chest of life.

We all need physical, mental, and spiritual abundance. You can find a certain level of physical abundance with any job that pays well. This is because you can afford what you need in order to live. However, finding a deeper level of abundance - physical, mental, and spiritual - requires finding a job and a line of work that spark your interest. Your interests are what you're naturally drawn to because you feel an intrinsic pull to study, understand, improve, and contribute to a specific product, service, or experience. Following your interests when choosing a job allows you to embody your interests and really live them each day.

Finally, when you work without understanding and connection to your impacts, your actions have more unseen, adverse effects on yourself, others, and the environment. Working against your own intentions for yourself, others, or the planet eventually builds up as anxiety and stress internally and externally. However, when you work in alignment with your interests, you know from first-hand experience that the products, services, or experiences you're providing are helping other people and the world. When you work in alignment with your interests, you'll feel that the energy and effort you're putting forth each day is of good use for yourself and others. This solves the work-life balance issues involving detachment from our impacts and lack of joy in the process of working. Your interests will reconnect you to the impacts of your actions, as well as your intrinsic motivation and joy, simply because you are working for a cause or mission that aligns with your interests.

Leading with your interests is essential for finding natural motivation to go to work each day, finding deeper abundance, and feeling that your effort is truly meaningful and impactful.

What keeps us from following our interests in the first place?

Before learning how you can understand and lead with your interests, let's talk about why so many people lose track of their own interests. Why is there such a disconnect between interests and work for so many people? Why doesn't each and every person work for an organization with products, services, or experiences that spark their interests?

To answer this question, you must return to your intention for doing work. **Intentions are what you want to be for yourself and others, what you aim to contribute, and the impact you hope to have on the world.** Everyone has an intention when embarking on a job search and choosing a line of work. It's surprising how often we're unaware of what our intentions *really* are. Recall a past or present job search of your own. What were your intentions and goals for your search? Your goal was probably to find a job. However, what was your intention for entering into that line of work and contributing?

Many people often get off-track when choosing a job because they don't connect to their interests and intentions. When it comes to choosing a job, the first approach most people take is to spend a lot of time building skills and knowledge that fulfill a current market need because that's what will land them a secure, high-paying job. Though it's typically a practical piece of advice to choose a job where you'll earn a living, this isn't the best primary intention. Why? You will feel empty and in autopilot mode quickly. If you have ever secured a job for the money, you probably know this already. Money does not guarantee genuine, sustainable motivation or deep abundance.

Also, market needs are fleeting and constantly changing. They are not predictable, especially in the world we live in today. Society changes quickly, far beyond our ability to comprehend or control. What is real, right now? What can you really know at any moment? Your interests. When you take the money-centric approach, you often reduce or limit your long-term abundance.

Another popular yet misguided approach is to accept a job because of the title or affiliation, while believing that it will lead somewhere better in the future. It feels good to tell someone you work for X company or have Y job title. This intention of acquiring more attention or the feeling achievement is also empty. Eventually we become addicted to the cycle of achievement and praise... with what outcome? This builds up our ego and it doesn't lead to genuine motivation, deep abundance, or connection with the meaning and impact of our work.

Over time, this ego-centered approach becomes really exhausting. When we finally look inward and ask what we're achieving and contributing each day, the purpose often isn't there. Identifying your interests prompts you to rewire the work-life balance approach by looking inward and asking yourself what your true interests really are. A job that aligns with your interests is the most valuable and impactful choice because you know inside that it is valuable and impactful.

Finally, another approach that leads many job seekers off track is simply lack of awareness. Many people simply don't have the time, space, or encouragement to consider their true interests when initially choosing a job. For some, getting a job can feel like an urgent process. A job is something many of us are simply led to by someone else or by life itself. We take whatever is out there and available. Some people get lucky and this grab-and-go approach works out; but much of the time we eventually find ourselves questioning what our work and life are really about when we don't lead with our interests. Luckily, you have the encouragement and guidance for tapping into your interests right now, with this book!

Now that you're aware of the obstacles that often get in the way of leading with your interests, it's time to learn how to actually understand and use your interests in the job search!

How can you lead with your interests?

Your interests are closely tied with your inherent personality traits and preferences. True interests are authentic and pure because they manifest without a lot of conditioning from other humans and society. This means that, rather than looking externally, look to yourself for answers.

First, identify your current interests. List what brings you joy, connection, and inspiration. Try naming these things as products, services, and experiences. You use many products and services every single day. You also engage in many experiences. What are the products and services that are most important to you and have changed your life for the better? What comes to mind when you think about daily essentials or larger positive life-changing experiences?

It's important to understand your interests, not just identify them. Next, think about why those products, services, and experiences really interest you. Why do they spark joy, connection, and inspiration? This can take time to think about and to articulate clear answers. In order to lead with your interests at work and in life, you must understand how your interests translate to specific impacts and feelings.

Finally, take action! Put your interests to use. When figuring out how you want to contribute, look at jobs that allow you to connect with and contribute in alignment with your interests. **Look for jobs within organizations that produce the products, services, and experiences that spark your interests.** This will provide intrinsic motivation to show up for work every day and give you a clear understanding about the impacts of your work. We'll explore these three steps further in the exercises.

It's Never Too Late

A quick note to those who might feel too far down the path to return to work that truly interests you. **It's never too late to lead with your interests at work and in life.** It is certainly easier to gain the support to follow and develop your interests at a young age, but it's never too late to reconnect with your interests. It is always the right decision to work in alignment with your interests.

Do you feel like you don't have any real interests anymore? Identifying your interests is sometimes very related to returning to your inner child. This is a great place to start. What you were drawn to as a kid, whether it's a certain experience, activity, or product, is very telling of where your authentic interests lie as an adult and what you feel is truly valuable for humanity. It takes work to identify your true interests and what are inauthentic, conditioned perceptions of value.

Though your youthful interests are often your most pure and authentic, your interests will change and evolve as you mature and gain experience. It is a continuous practice to tune into your interests. You must find the practices that help you become an observer of yourself to remain connected to your present interests and work in alignment with them. When you awaken to the fact that the only way is to lead with your interests, your life will become more full of ease and enthusiasm.

How I Reconnected with my Interests

In high school, during the summers, I worked as a camp counselor. I loved teaching and giving kids experiences that opened their realm of awareness, knowledge, and potential. I enjoyed explaining concepts, designing creative exercises for students, and presenting information. While teaching, I also learned a lot about myself and my interests.

Teaching was a job I did purely out of interest. I didn't show up only for the money, recognition, or because someone told me to. I woke up excited to go to work. It was an experience that evoked joy, connection, and inspiration. I saw and felt the positive impacts on all levels.

Of course, as a young adult, my interests weren't all as serious and career-oriented as teaching. When I was in high school, one of my favorite pastimes was shopping. I loved going to the mall to discover new products and find inspiration. It was a place to kick back, catch up with friends, and explore after a long week of school pressure and structure. I always visited specific stores that had new decorations and products to discover. While discovering new products in a retail environment, I felt happy and inspired. The products were not just about labels and image; they were functional, made me happy day-to-day, and inspired me creatively.

However, when it was time to choose a college and a field of study, I did not lead with my interests in teaching and retail. Why? Well, shopping doesn't sound like a major that exists at all, let alone worth pursuing. Family and teachers told me that following market needs and building skills that promised a high financial return was the right path to follow. I was encouraged to do something that leveraged my talents in math and science. So, I pursued a rigorous, challenging academic path that promised to lead to achievement, financial success, and job security. I studied engineering and business in college.

At the time, I felt that I was interested in both engineering and business. Looking back, I was actually disconnected from my true core interests. I was more interested in approval and security. The desire for praise and achievement was talking louder than my own internal voice. I was somewhat aware of my true interests, but I didn't think about the possibility of a connection between my personal interests, my education, and my career. I was operating in a work-life balance mindset. It didn't occur to me that I should think independently about my education instead of following advice and job market statistics. So, I initially kept my interests and my work aspirations in separate silos.

In college, whenever I had time off from the rigor of engineering classes, I gravitated back to shopping. I always wanted to see what new products were available and how the stores prepared for each new season. I also gravitated back to teaching. Instead of traveling or taking time off during school vacations, I found teaching jobs. This kind of work fed my spirit and my stomach. I never felt resistance or questioned why I went shopping or why I sought out teaching jobs. It's just what I did whenever I had time and focus to spend outside of school.

Meanwhile, during my first year of engineering school, I became very stressed and anxious. The rigor of engineering school and the competitive environment took a toll on my mental health. Even though I was leveraging my natural talents for math and science, I wasn't motivated or interested. I felt resistance, which was really an inner misalignment. My studies and work direction were separate from my personal interests. I had to get my studies "over with" in order to deserve some time for my personal interests, joy, and genuine inspiration. I woke up with little motivation to conquer the challenge of engineering schoolwork and enter into a life-long career in something I wasn't personally motivated to pursue.

I started looking for help to resolve my pain and frustration. I read articles about how to self-motivate. I considered switching majors. Luckily, help arrived in my e-mail inbox in the form of a Groupon offer. I took advantage of the Groupon offer and took my first-ever yoga class. I didn't know what to expect at all, but I needed something different to get moving and out of my comfort zone, away from the school environment.

After that first class, I realized that the yoga practice boosted my confidence and my strength. It was exactly what I needed. The yoga studio gave me a place to find mental space, connect to my own internal voice, and practice self-inquiry. The yoga studio became my oasis away from school where I could reconnect with my breath and exercise in a way that rejuvenated my body and my mind. Teachers offered questions from yoga philosophy, that prompted me to ask myself about my purpose and true interests. This was where I worked on alignment between my professional development and personal growth. I started my journey toward work-life integration.

I returned to college for my second year of engineering school. Even though it was only the fall semester, other students in my class were already interviewing for summer internships at large engineering firms and investment banks. Instead of following external advice, I thought about what I really wanted in a summer internship. With my newfound strength and internal voice, I thought about my approach to seeking an internship of my own. I could go back to teaching or look for an internship that reflected what I was learning in engineering school… or something else?

As I continued to practice yoga, make more decisions for myself, and write about my interests and intentions, I felt more confident. The conditioned layers between my authentic interests and my actions melted away. I could hear my own voice of reason without immediately reaching out for external advice or guidance. Nothing obvious shifted immediately. I stayed in engineering school. However, given this new mindset and approach, my actions led down a very different path. I kept an open mind and considered a variety of work options.

The fall turned to winter and the holidays were approaching. One Saturday morning while window shopping in the city after a yoga class, I was thinking about what I would do for work over winter break. I had never worked in retail but I decided that I would apply to work in a store. I walked into my favorite store in the city and asked the manager if they were hiring temporary workers for the winter holidays. She said yes, and then she asked if I was a student. I told her that I was. She told me that the corporate office was currently looking for students for the company's summer intern program. She encouraged me to apply online. It was as if she had read my mind! - As if she knew the summer internship was a looming worry on my mind. But what would an engineering student do in a retail company?

When I got back to my dorm, I looked online and found a long list of intern positions on the company's website. I even found a supply chain internship that required engineering skills. Was this real? Could I really work as an engineer in retail? I didn't care about the position or the work I'd be doing as much as the fact that **I had found an opportunity that aligned with my interests.** I was sold. It was the hardest I had ever worked on an application but it was worth it because, two months later, I won the summer intern position! I felt a sense of calm and joy. I knew I was following the path to work-life integration.

That summer was one of my best. I had found work that aligned with my interests. I showed up to work engaged and motivated to learn and contribute. I learned about the behind-the-scenes inner workings of a retail company. I found ways of contributing that leveraged my skills. I learned a lot about myself too; in terms of what tasks I enjoyed doing and the skills to work in this field. It was an experience of applied learning that formed the foundation for a career in alignment with my interests, even if unconventional and tangent to the conveyor belt of my formal education.

With this new perspective on work, I felt freed of the constraints of formal education and society. I had the power to lead with my interests both at work and outside of work. **I could make an impact that was meaningful to me, and this provided unlimited intrinsic motivation to work.** Even now, over 10 years later, I realize how the decision to follow my interests led to greater contribution, happiness, connection, and creativity.

The world is exciting because each of us has a unique set of interests. We need people interested in food. We need people interested in design. We need people interested in music. We need people interested in the environment. We need people interested in writing. We need it all!

Interests

in Action

Interests Exercises

Many people go through the motions of each day and lose sight of their true interests. You're lucky if you have friends and family that ask you about your interests and encourage you to pursue work in alignment with your interests.

Once you tap into your interests - the products, services, and experiences that evoke happiness, connection, and inspiration for you, then it is time to begin your job search. In the three Interests exercises, you'll learn how to identify your true interests and begin your job search. Work through the exercises with care. Take your time and enjoy.

Exercise 1: Map Your Interests

Exercise 2: Hone in on a Focus

Exercise 3: Find an Application

Supplies:

- Pen or pencil
- Paper
- Journal
- Black, red, green, blue, and orange pens (or pencils)

Interests

Exercise 1: Map Your Interests

Intention: Reconnect with what makes you feel connected, happy, and inspired in order to lead with your interests when searching for a job.

In this exercise, you will map your interests (work and life interests) using mind mapping! Mind Mapping is a tool for organizing and articulating information. A mind map is a visual diagram that displays information efficiently, in a way that shows connections. The process of mind mapping is expansive and allows you to brainstorm, organize, and see important connections.

In this exercise, you'll make your Interests Map to tap into your true interests. Later on, you'll learn how to use this map to search for jobs that are in alignment with your interests. Remember that choosing a job in alignment with your interests allows you to learn more about your interests and understand the positive impact of your work.

Let's get started. On the opposite page, I have provided an example of an Interests Map. Notice how the expansive nature of a mind map allows for ideating and brainstorming your interests. Turn the page to begin making your own Interests Map!

in Action

Example of a Completed Interests Map

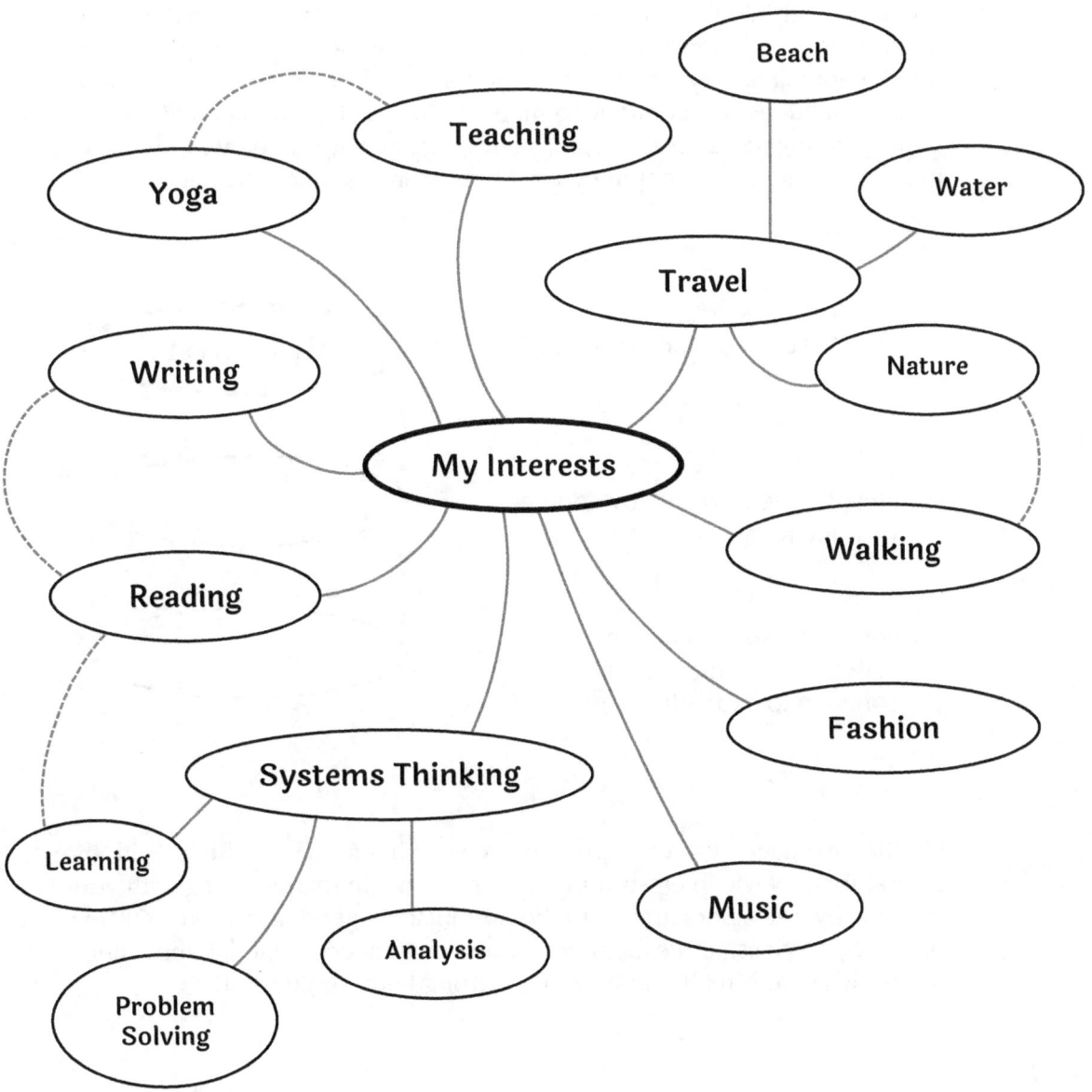

Interests

Exercise 1: Map Your Interests

To make your Interests Map, simply start with a central topic (in this case, My Interests) and then begin to branch by free associating. The process of mind mapping is very simple, but your map will become more valuable and impactful as you continue to map and layer. The template with the basic ordering ideas, or layers, for your Interests Map is below. Use this map as guidance for mapping your interests on the following page.

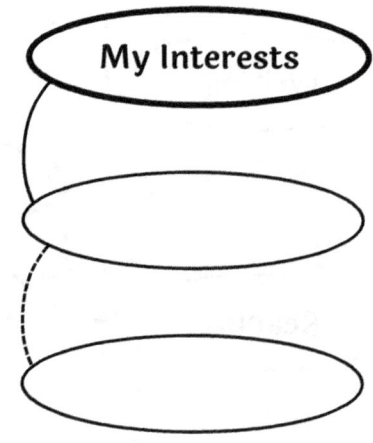

Step 1. Focus on the central topic

Step 2. Free associate by adding your interests

Step 3. Make connections between your interests and continue to expand!

On the next page, it's your turn to make your interests map. Begin with the central topic of My Interests and, from there, begin reconnecting with your interests by free associating with the prompts: What are my interests? What products, services, and experiences make me feel connected, happy, and inspired? There is really no way to go wrong here, so go for it!

in Action

Exercise 1: Map Your Interests

Your turn!

Interests

Exercise 2: Hone in on a Focus

Intention: Use your Interests Map to hone in on the interests that you want to engage with at work and learn more about.

Most of us have a variety of interests. After identifying your true interests, how do you actually use this information to navigate your job search? That is what this second exercise is all about.

The goal of this second exercise is to evaluate which interests you really want to learn more about and engage day-to-day. The result of this exercise is a clear awareness of your interests that align with your strengths, learning objectives, and curiosity.

In this exercise, you'll use color (or symbols, if you prefer) to identify the best interests to lead with when navigating the job search.

Begin with Step 1.

Step 1: To get started, prepare 4 different color markers or highlighters. I suggest using the colors red, blue, green, and yellow to have maximum contrast. If you don't have colored markers, choose four different symbols. I would suggest using a circle dot, a square, a triangle, and a star.

View the color version of this exercise at:
www.awakeleadershipsolutions.com/awake-apprentice-exercises
Password: Apprent!ce

Exercise 2: Hone in on a Focus

Step 2: Return to your Interests Map from Exercise 1. Categorize your map using the 4 colors (or 4 symbols you have chosen).

Red: Interests as a child, or interests from the past

Blue: Current interests

Green: Interests that speak to your current strengths

Orange: Interests that you want to learn more about

Refer to the example on the following page.

Interests

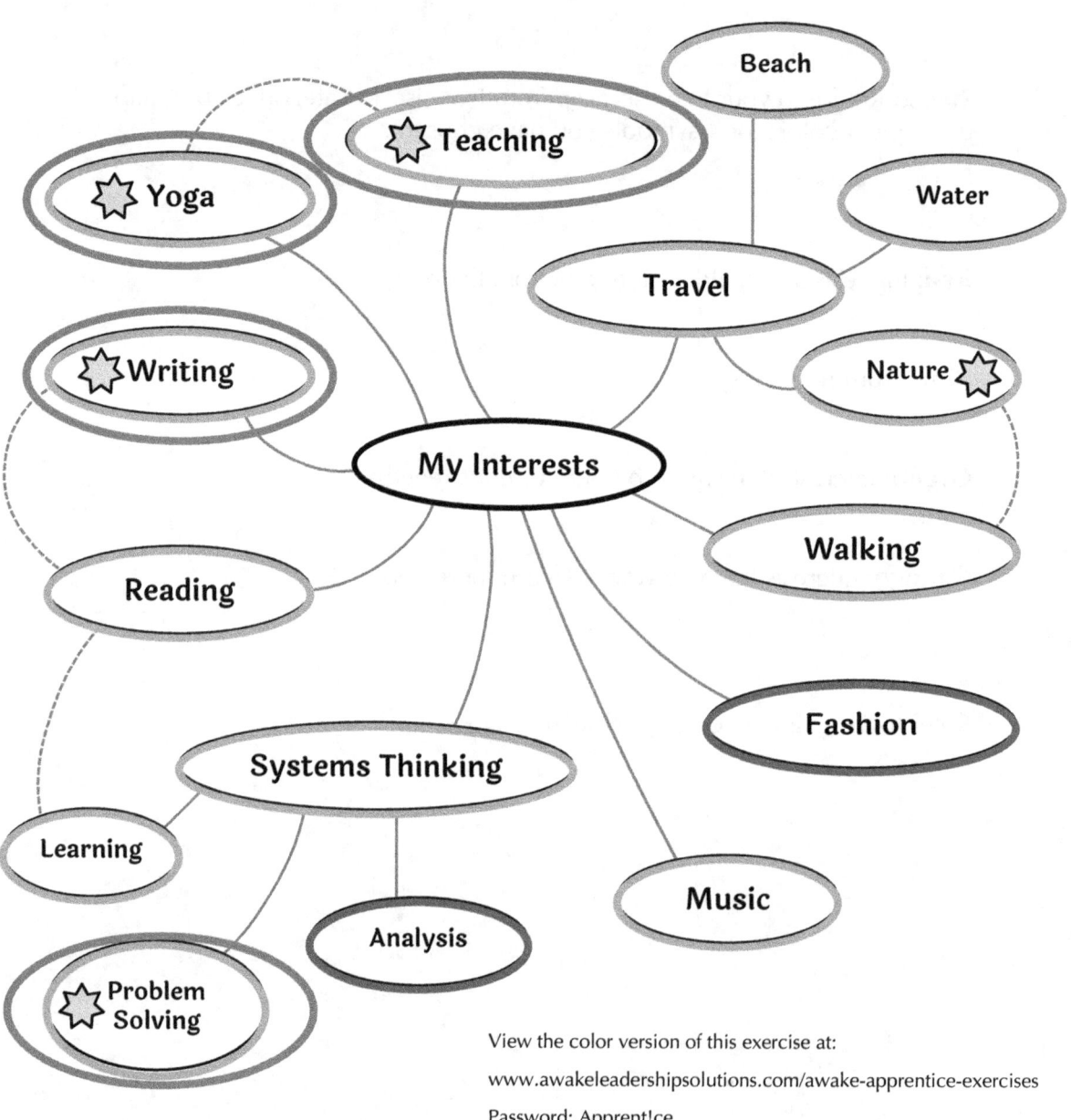

Example of a Completed Interests Map

View the color version of this exercise at:
www.awakeleadershipsolutions.com/awake-apprentice-exercises
Password: Apprent!ce

in Action

Exercise 2: Hone in on a Focus

Step 3: Once you have color-coded your map, take a step back and notice:

How many **current** interests do you have (blue)? Answer: _____

How many of your current interests also align with your **current** strengths (blue and green)? Answer: _____

How many of your current interests do you want to **learn** more about (blue and orange)? Answer: _____

How many of your current interests align with your strengths and spark your **curiosity** (blue, green, and orange)? Answer: _____

If you want to make any changes or additions to your map after doing this exercise once, that's fine! Go back and do that. However, it's also important to keep in mind what emerged during your first attempt because this is what is at the forefront of your mind!

In this exercise, you narrowed down your search to a more focused, specific set of interests. In the next and final exercise of the chapter, you'll use this work to learn how to leverage this color-coded map to navigate your job search.

Interests

Exercise 3: Find an Application

Intention: *Use your color-coded Interests Map to find a job that aligns with your interests.*

Now it's time to apply what you have worked on so far to your job search! In this exercise, you'll use your color-coded Interests Map to identify the **key words** to use when searching for your experience of applied learning (your job). You'll also use this deeper understanding of your interests to facilitate conversations and inquire with intention.

What companies and organizations can you work for that offer products or services in alignment with your interests? Who can you connect with through your personal network, LinkedIn, or friends and family that could give you more information about how to find jobs in these fields?

When searching for a job, or experience of applied learning, it's most important to choose interests from your map that are in alignment with something you want to learn more about. For example, an interest in writing could translate to working at a publishing house, becoming a journalist, or becoming an author.

These can be past or present interests. Also, they don't have to necessarily reflect a current strength you have. Why? You can always build new strengths and capabilities. However, I have found that the best candidates for a field of work align with your current interests, reflect a current strength, and spark your curiosity.

Get started: Refer to your color-coded interests map. Follow the prompts to begin your search. You can use a journal to expand on your answers to the questions.

in Action

Exercise 3: Find an Application

Look at the interests (past and present) on your Interests Map that are in alignment with your **learning** interests and spark your **curiosity.** What types of jobs do these interests translate to? Cast a wide net here and brainstorm! Answering this question might require online research, an informal job search, or a talk with an expert or a wise friend.

Interests

Exercise 3: Find an Application

Using your previous answer: <u>Why</u> do you want to **learn** more about these interests? What type of job sparks your **curiosity**? As you saw in my story, I wanted to learn more about the retail world because I was a customer and I was curious about the inner-workings of the retail industry.

in Action

Exercise 3: Find an Application

You now have a clearer picture of what your interests are, which interests you want to learn more about and engage with, and the type of jobs that you can explore and apply for. Here is some additional guidance for navigating your job search.

1. Conduct your search! Research and explore jobs in alignment with your interests. Return to your Interests Map regularly during your search.

2. Seek out advice and information. Search for information from online forums, as well as respected friends, peers, and experts.

3. Apply and interview! Start with applying for jobs that also reflect your current strengths.

4. Keep growing and learning. If a job aligns with your interests and sparks your curiosity but doesn't reflect your current strengths, think about how you could build the strengths or capabilities prior, look for a similar job that reflects your strengths, or commit to building those strengths early on when you start the job.

5. Voice your interest. Remember to voice your interest when inquiring or applying! Use your answers from the exercises in this chapter to express your intention.

6. Talk to people and ask questions! When interviewing, ask about the mission, a typical day at work, and advice about how to succeed in the position.

Good luck with your search. Turn the page for one final quick tip. Then, we'll dive into Chapter 2, Possibility, which is all about finding a job with the right support.

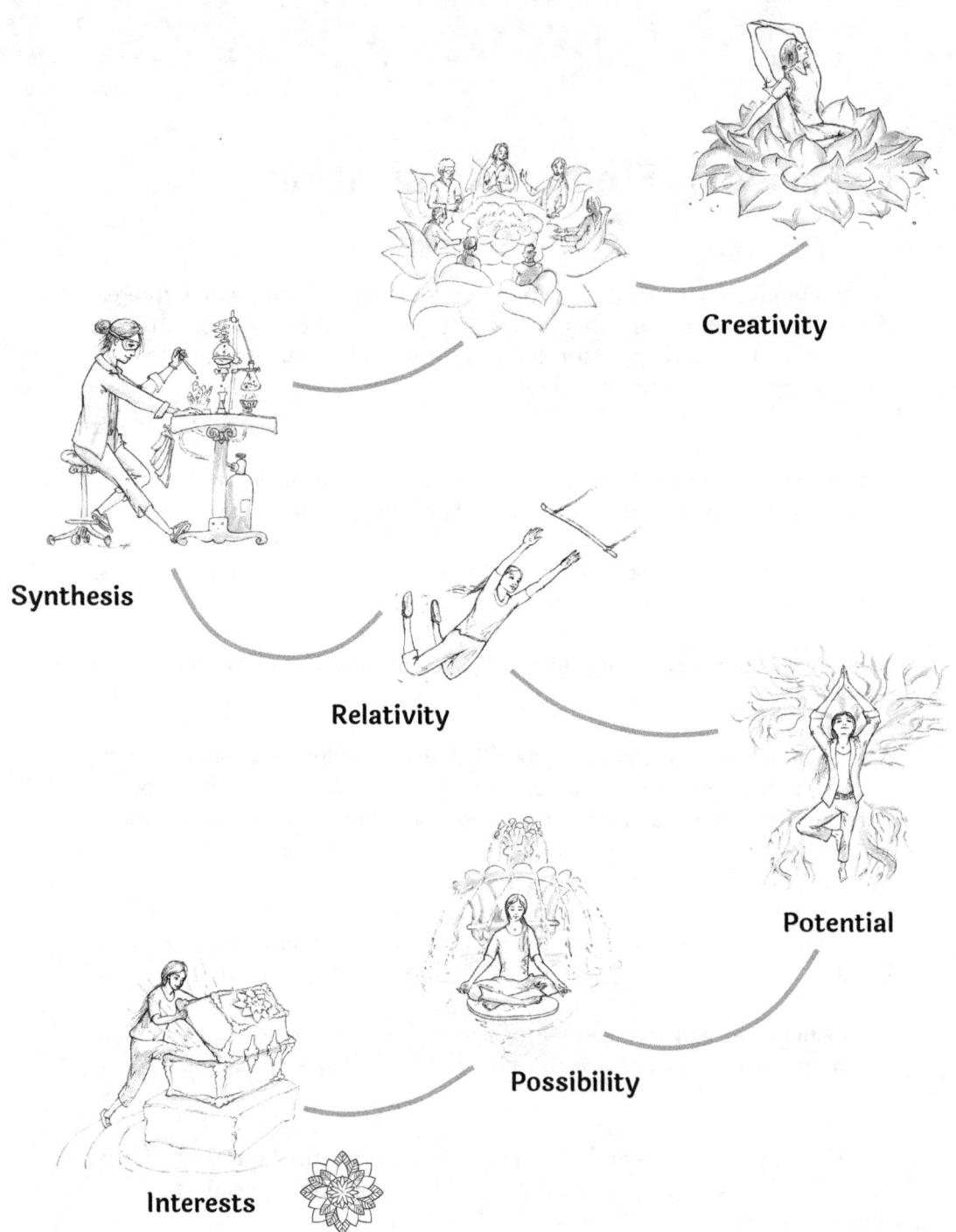

Earth to Creative Leader Tip #1

Lead with Ethical Interests

When chosing an interest to lead with in your job search and your work, here is some guidance to keep in mind!

Ethics are principles for moral behavior. Ethics guide us as to how we should behave toward ourselves and toward others in order to find a balance of peace and progress. As I explain in the *Awake Ethics* guidebook, acting ethically results in providing the most good for others, yourself, and the world in any situation. Ethical interests have an impact that provides more good than harm. Ideally, they don't cause any harm at all.

Sometimes, we have interests in things that are harmful to our physical or mental health. These are usually temporary interests that we may be attracted to out of conditioning. They inflate our ego and provide temporary comfort or pleasure. Sometimes, we have interests in things that actually harm other people or harm the environment. Seek deeper awareness before taking action based on an interest. **Follow interests that maximize the good for yourself, others, and the world.** When following an interest and pursuing a job, choose an interest that has ethical impacts on yourself, other people, and the world.

Up Next...

You might be thinking that leading with your interests sounds great in theory, but what about salary and basic support at work? Aren't these things important when searching for a job? They are! **In Chapter 2, we'll explore Possibility**, which is all about finding a job that also offers the right support.

Chapter 2
Possibility

Fill the Fountain of Possibility

After identifying job options that align with your interests, it is important to choose a job that also offers an abundance of **possibility**. Your interests should be the primary driver of abundance for you at work; however, without possibility, following your interests is often not possible. Many people find jobs they love but later find that certain essential aspects of support are lacking.

A fountain cannot work without water in the reservoir. An Awake Apprentice cannot work without the right elements of possibility in place. **We all need energy and specific resources in order to produce quality work and to enjoy the process of working.** I'm talking about things like a salary, a place to live, and a schedule that supports your health. What are the tangible things that make it possible for you to go to work each day and sustain at a given organization?

I have found that there are six basic elements of possibility to consider when searching for the right job. The six essential elements of possibility are: an offer, money, people, culture, environment, and schedule. These elements are the aspects of a job that allow you to do your best work each day. In this chapter, we'll talk about the elements of possibility and how to identify which elements of possibility are most critical for you when searching for a new job opportunity.

Possibility needs cross over between our work and our personal life. Your work life and personal life are inherently connected and inform each other. It is important to cultivate the conditions for possibility both at work and outside of work in order to fuel your best work and life. What many people don't realize, especially early on in their career, is that we each need different kinds of possibility.

It takes deep reflection and **Self-study** to really know the elements of possibility that you need in order to do your best work. At the beginning of your career, it's often a period of trial

A fountain does not work without water in the reservoir.
An Awake Apprentice cannot work without the right elements
of possibility in place.

and error. You learn what works and what doesn't through experience. Then, you choose jobs that are more in alignment with your specific needs based on your past learnings. Many people accept what they are offered from a company or organization and try to adapt. However, this isn't sustainable. Each person has inherent needs for possibility and you can only truly succeed as an Awake Apprentice when you find a job that closely aligns with your needs for possibility.

This chapter is about really understanding your needs and cultivating a deeper sense of self-awareness. Self-awareness will enable you to take greater control over your choices and set yourself up with greater confidence and success when choosing a job offer. When you know more of what you need in a job, you're more likely to seek out and choose a job that fulfills your possibility needs. We'll also talk about how to remedy the elements of possibility if you find that there is a lack at any point, in order to save the possibility at your job.

A responsible Awake Apprentice is aware of his or her possibility needs and considers the elements of possibility when evaluating a job opportunity. Part of finding the right job is finding an organization and team that offers possibility for you at this time in your career. This chapter will give you the opportunity to reflect on the elements of possibility and prompt you to proactively reflect on your ideal conditions for your job.

The Six Elements of Possibility

The six elements of possibility are the sustenance you need in order to thrive at work. Just as the earth exists and functions in the form of elements (earth, water, air, fire, and ether), an Awake Apprentice has essential elements for possibility. The six elements of Possibility are: **an opportunity, a salary, a supportive leadership team, a conducive environment, a healthy schedule, and a compatible culture**. All of these elements are important for a successful work experience. If one of these elements is lacking, it is often impossible to continue to work and make progress.

These six elements of possibility are necessary considerations for all apprentices; however, the importance of each element differs for each person. It takes time to learn what elements of possibility are most important for you. Let's take a closer look at the six elements of possibility and how to cultivate the conditions for each element. These are things to evalutae closely as you go through the interview and offer process.

Element 1: An Offer

The first basic element of possibility is an offer. This seems pretty obvious but you do need an offer before starting a new job. There must be a need, a customer, and resources before embarking on your new apprenticeship. **A job opportunity and an offer are the springboard for your apprenticeship.**

When evaluating an opportunity, consider whether it aligns with your true interests. Using your Interests Map, decide if the context and impact really align with your interests. Also consider if you have the right skills and strengths for the job. Prioritize opportunities on your list that align with your current qualifications but also challenge you to stretch past your current comfort zone.

If the job description doesn't give you a clear picture of the skills and strengths necessary, as well as what you will learn, you can call or e-mail the organization to ask questions about the position. The interview is also an ideal time to get first-hand insight from your future leader about what skills you need and what skills you'll build.

Has anyone ever landed a job that didn't already have a job posting associated with it? Yes. If you start using your interests map to search for jobs and you can't find a title or description that exactly matches your criteria, search more broadly. Search for organizations where your skills could come in handy. Call or e-mail to ask if they could use someone with your skills and interests. It never hurts to ask. However, even after successfully creating a job opportunity for yourself, there has to ultimately be an official job offer.

Element 2: Salary

Money is an essential part of fueling your work and your life. No matter how much you may want to barter or remove yourself from the money system all together (and believe me, I have been there), money is deeply ingrained into the fabric of our society. It has good uses and bad uses.

Money is useful for quantifying value and energy. We need money to pay rent, eat healthy food, and enjoy special experiences. However, money can take on artificial value very easily based on influence, addiction, and past conditioning. Fortunately, by leading with your interests, money becomes a sideline supporter instead of a central driver for your work. Money allows you to obtain the resources you need to do your best work and thrive as an apprentice. **It's best to view salary as something that fuels your best work and your best life.** This will ensure that you have what you need. This will also serve as a starting point for determining the salary you need and negotiating your salary.

When considering if the salary offered is enough for you, the first thing to note is that your time is priceless. Humanity has put a number value on time for certain types of work and contributions; however, in reality, our time is priceless. It's true.

Your life and your time don't have a real dollar value. We all have a demand for more time and there is an unknown supply. Your time is constantly diminishing and **how you choose to spend each moment is really what makes you who you are.** This is why it is essential to lead with your interests! No matter how much money you are offered, the opportunity to focus on your interests each day is priceless.

How you spend your time is how you build your identity. Working on something that aligns with your interests is the best way to spend your work time. Our time is far too valuable to work on a process or result that has no value to us intrinsically. Seek opportunities that allow you to spend your time now in a way that you enjoy, and pave the way to enjoy your time even more in the future. Hopefully this perspective helps you to zoom out and see salary not as the primary driver for taking a job, but as the supporting fuel. Let's now take a closer look at what an abundant salary really looks like.

Most job seekers search for jobs that align with their qualifications, years of experience, and market worth. They then conform their personal financial needs to fit this amount that they "deserve". Most people accept and adapt to the salary that is offered to them. I find it sad that so many people believe that they are "worth" a certain dollar amount and therefore deserve a fixed amount of resources. *I'm worth X so I deserve Y. Given what I'm worth at my job, I can afford this or that.* This is not only unrealistic, since we each have different needs based on our personal support needs, but it also takes our focus away from so many of the things in life that really matter like the impacts of our work, our experience, and our relationships with others.

If you determine your salary needs based on what you believe you are worth on the market, you will eliminate great apprenticeship opportunities. There is a better way to determine what you are worth and what you deserve. Again, instead of looking outward for answers about our worth, it's about looking inward!

First and foremost, to determine the salary that you need and deserve, practice Self-Study. **Self-study is the practice of observing and becoming aware of your true interests, needs, and desires.** Your perception of what you need is often based on your past conditioning and influences. Depending on how you were raised during your childhood, you might be attached to certain products, services, and experiences that you really don't need in your adult life. Sometimes the things people spend money on really don't support their best work and life. So many people live in excess. Without knowing your needs, it's hard to know if you'll be paid enough to thrive. You need to do the Self-Study to identify the elements that truly allow you to thrive.

So, the first step is to evaluate and quantify your true needs. *What do you truly need? What are some things you could let go of in order to feel more free and choose a job in alignment with your interests?* As you'll see in my story, I found early on in my career that I didn't need as many material possessions as I thought. Next, quantify your needs in dollar terms per month and per year by using your past spending reports. *What do you need on a monthly basis financially? What do you need on an annual basis financially?*

Once you really are in tune with your needs, the secondary consideration is about how much you deserve. The reality is that, for the money system to work, you must provide value in order for your organization and leader to pay you. After all of your Self-Study work, how do you ultimately determine the salary you need to ask for? **Take an honest look at the value you would (or you currently do) provide for the organization.** Looking clearly at the value you provide for the organization and the customers can inform how the organization should be able and willing to compensate you. The value a role contributes is often subjective and hard to determine because all roles in a business are related and dependent on each other.

Choosing an opportunity in alignment with your interests will likely result in a higher salary offer because your dedication and passion will come through during the interview. You will be more productive and positive with the team. If the job pays far lower than you believe you deserve based on the value you would contribute, ask more about the position. The position may be titled differently than you're used to and it may be a lower-level job than you're actually looking for or qualified for. You can also ask for more money to meet your needs. Beyond hourly jobs, most salaries are flexible if you'll deliver the value. To recap, answer these questions:

1. What are your true financial needs on an annual basis? Include everything from your rent or mortgage to your family vacations and savings goals. This will give you your total base salary needs.

2. What is the value that you provide for your team, for the organization, and for customers? If you can get your head around this number, this will give you an idea of whether your base salary needs are realistic and if your salary could even be a bit higher based on your monetary value-add for the organization.

Money is important. There is no denying that money is our society's system for exchanging the resources we need to feel supported and do our best work for others. However, if you prioritize money over interests, you might be mistaking financial abundance for true abundance. Once you're over the initial high of getting paid, you'll realize it's really a gateway for bigger, more meaningful experiences and freedom.

Don't judge the abundance of an opportunity purely based on the salary number. Practice Self-study when determining your true financial needs. Also consider the value you would provide for the organization. These two benchmarks will also give you more negotiating power, in terms of clear reasoning, when negotiating salary.

Use salary considerations and negotiations as an opportunity to gain strength and confidence, as well as to set yourself up for success at work. Now, let's look at the third element of possibility: Leadership!

Element 3: Leadership

Before I dive into the qualities and actions that reflect great leadership, let's first answer the question: *Why choose a job where you have a leader?*

There are many modern job opportunities that offer work without the direct supervision of a leader. These jobs are especially prevalent in the gig economy. Contractors now use apps as their leaders. Many people find work to do online that involves no human interaction at all. Sometimes, reporting to someone and working with them in person feels limiting and frustrating. *Why not just be your own boss right away and avoid the hassle of having a leader at all?*

Having a leader is an essential aspect of an Awake Apprentice's work experience because having the guidance of an experienced leader gives you deeper expertise, confidence, and motivation. **Without work experience and guidance from an experienced leader, you lose the opportunity to learn from someone a little further down the path.** You lose the opportunity to gain first-hand knowledge, cultivate discipline, and receive mentorship and feedback that will amplify your strengths and capabilities. Finding a leader and leadership team that you respect and can learn from is an essential part of possibility for Awake Apprentices.

The qualities of a great leader depend on the team and each leader-apprentice relationship. Some universal qualities of great leaders are transparency, positivity, and clarity of vision. A leader should be able to give clear direction so that you are aware of your responsibilities and objectives. The leader sets the tone for the team culture and therefore should be positive and solution-centric. They should provide constructive feedback and positive acknowledgement that help you build confidence and strength. You should be able to cultivate a relationship of trust with your leader. Finally, a leader should be mentorial. Since an apprenticeship is all about learning and development, a great leader provides attention, learning opportunities, and knowledge. The right leader will be someone you respect and look forward to working with each day.

Just like other aspects of possibility, it's hard to know if your prospective leader will be ideal for you until you actually work together. Even if they talk the talk during the interview process, you don't really know if they are a great leader until you work together. True leadership strength is shown over time, especially in the toughest of times. However, this awareness is important during the interview process, as you feel out the vibe and style of different leaders.

The leader-apprentice relationship is a cornerstone of the apprentice experience. Beyond skills, knowledge, and support, a great leader provides learning opportunities. Since an apprenticeship is all about learning and development, this piece is essential. Having someone else to mentor and motivate you along your path makes the apprenticeship experience enriching and fulfilling. Great leaders inspire apprentices to do the same; to use their skills, knowledge, and time to help new apprentices feel supported and grow. Find a leader whom you respect, enjoy working with, and learn from. Your leader is your most important relationship in your apprenticeship.

If you want to experience working with your potential future leader before accepting a job, an internship is one way to work with a prospective leader and learn about the leadership style you like. You'll learn what kind of leadership style fuels your best work and what leadership qualities you aspire to embody. Find the right leader in order to fill the well of possibility.

Zooming out a bit further, the top-level leadership in an organization is also a factor that determines the quality of your possibility at work. The top-level leadership has control over budgets, hiring of important positions, and the cultural direction of the organization. The top-level leadership should be ethical, compassionate, and build relationships of trust and respect. If the top-level leadership does not value ethics and they are not dedicated to the mission of the company, you'll also feel lack of meaning and support. If the top-level leadership does not provide a clear vision, this will reflect throughout the organization and you will feel a lack of focus and direction.

During the search and interview process, make sure to evaluate the top-level leadership. Internet-based research about the leadership team and public reviews on platforms like Glassdoor are helpful directional information. Of course, the best way to gauge the leadership team is through work experience and reflection over time.

Element 4: Culture

Culture is a company's collective personality. Though culture is often talked about in terms of qualities, a company's cultural qualities are defined by specific behaviors and actions taken each day. **Culture is an element of possibility because culture has a big impact on your ability to focus and collaborate successfully at work.** Since work in an apprenticeship involves collaboration and interpersonal work, the behavioral qualities of the team and personalities make a big difference in your ability to succeed! The top-level leadership is the key influencer of culture at any organization. However, the culture of any organization is the sum of every individual's behaviors and actions.

Since interests are the driving force for Awake Apprentices when choosing a job opportunity, a compatible company culture is usually one where other employees share your interests for the product, service, or experience. If you share genuine interest in the company's mission and vision, then collaboration will be more seamless and drama-free.

Cultural qualities that stem from a collective mission result in practices and shared values that reflect the company's values and priorities. The company Patagonia values the environment and environmental activism, so employees are encouraged to get outside and surf during breaks. The company Blue Bottle is aligned around the mission to provide great quality coffee, so employees receive a free pound of coffee every week. These perks and shared practices are a reflection of values and build culture. If you choose an opportunity in alignment with your interests, the culture is more likely to align as well.

Culture is also cultivated through subtler practices and habits found in behaviors in interactions. The leadership often sets the example for behavior in meetings and one-on-one interactions, but each person is responsible for setting a positive example. Many people speak of "positive company culture" but don't specify what that really means in action. Seemingly small but important behaviors like listening in meetings, giving positive acknowledgement, and saying "thank you" are cultural norms that make a big difference day-to-day and result in a positive, respectful culture. Behaviors like using a negative tone, giving harsh criticism, and political talk and drama are cultural norms that can be distracting and make a job experience painful. We go through our busy days taking in all of these subtler behaviors but rarely reflect on which behaviors and habits are really building the culture we want to see and live each day. Think about how you will feel respected and be respectful each day at your prospective place of work.

How can you gauge if the culture is right for you and will fuel your best work? **When you go for an interview or an on-site visit, ask questions and observe.** Ask questions to gauge people's connection to the mission and genuine interests. Ask about what they value about the company culture most. It's challenging to fully grasp the cultural tone and norms through an interview or on-site visit, but observing people and feeling the energy is often the best way to gauge culture. *Do you feel comfortable? Do people seem happy? Do you feel inspired? Do you feel free? Do you feel like this is somewhere you want to show up to everyday?* When evaluating a job, assessing culture is often more about feeling than analyzing.

Just like traveling to a different country, sometimes it's helpful to immerse in a completely different culture in order to understand what cultural qualities fuel your best work. We'll talk more about this in the Relativity chapter. Different experiences will help you learn more about yourself, your ability to adapt, and your true preferences. As you experience different work cultures, you'll learn what preferences you have and what workplace energy really makes you thrive. You'll pick up on the little things that matter. *Do people say hello and smile at each other? Is the workspace clean? Do people seem to respect you, your work, and the organization?* These are things to consider as you interview.

The next element of possibility, Environment, is closely related to culture.

Element 5: Environment

Whether you work at an office, a coffee shop, or from home, your work environment has a huge effect on the process and the results of your work. An ideal work environment allows you to balance focused solo work time and collaborative time. A great work environment has positive energy. **Each person has different environmental preferences depending on his or her role and personal needs.**

Just as you learn what conditions you need for a sustainable salary and living space at home, you often learn what your ideal work environment is (and isn't) based on your experience, especially early in your career. You'll start to gain awareness of what fuels your best work and what your parameters are for an ideal environment.

Until I experienced it, I had never realized that things like a dog-friendly policy could have such an impact on my day-to-day experience and ability to focus. Though I love dogs, dogs in my work environment definitely did not enhance my productivity or mood overall. However, I found that a community café was a great addition to an office environment. At my first job, there was an awesome café with coffee, juices, and snacks. It was a great place for co-workers to meet and take a break. It was a lifesaver when you needed a pick-me-up to continue working and didn't have time to drive off campus. I missed this a lot at my second company, which did not have a café.

While these may not sound like deal-breakers, the environment is definitely worth considering when evaluating a job opportunity. It's helpful to know your must-have's for your work environment. *Do you want to work in a city office or on a farm? Do you want a bike-friendly commute? Do you need silence?*

Do you need white noise? Do you need natural light? What is your ideal work environment?

Once you have your ideal work environment terms in mind, it's much easier to evaluate if you'll be successful day-to-day at your apprenticeship. When you interview, try to get onsite and see where you'll be working to evaluate if the environment is right for you and fuels your best work.

Work environments are also changeable and often negotiable, too. With technology, the ability to work remotely has become easier and more widely accepted. Companies work hard to retain employees by accommodating specific requests and preferences. *What changes to your current work environment would enhance your ability to focus? What changes would make the environment more inspiring?*

If you can, it's often helpful to work from different locations to remain inspired and energetic. Even working from a different room or changing your view can make a positive difference. As I mentioned earlier, we often assume that the conditions we inherit when we join an organization are fixed and we must accept them. However, part of cultivating your own possibility in order to do your best work is to bring awareness to what you need in order to do your best work. If you feel that your work environment could benefit from a change, don't be afraid to ask your leader.

Let's now look at the sixth and final element of possibility: Schedule.

Element 6: Schedule

The final element of possibility is your work schedule. Work schedules vary based on the organization and the job. Some positions require a more rigid, fixed work schedule and others are more flexible. Many people don't evaluate a job opportunity based on the work schedule expectations; however, your work schedule impacts one of the most important factors for success in an apprenticeship: your health. **Without health and energy, it's impossible to do your best work.**

Some work schedules require long or strange hours and extensive travel. Taking on a job where the work schedule affects your sleep schedule or ability to practice self-care can have detrimental effects both during your peak working years and later on in life. Without sleep, you will get sick more often and lose your ability to focus. Your productivity will decline and you'll jeopardize your own success. Even if a job looks ideal, if the schedule does not support your health and self-care needs, it will be impossible to succeed and enjoy the experience. Before considering a job, take a close look at the schedule requirements and expectations. The work schedule is a serious consideration when evaluating job options.

The right work schedule can actually have a positive impact on both your health and your happiness if it provides the right balance of structure and flexibility. If you thrive when you have a scheduled a routine, take on an apprenticeship that provides a structured, consistent schedule. If an apprenticeship has a very structured, clear schedule, make sure it fuels your best work or that you're open to adapting to it.

On the other hand, if you prefer a more freeform schedule or a schedule that changes, look for a job that provides more flexibility for you to design your own hours. Or, choose a job where the work schedule changes seasonally. If you take on a work schedule that goes against your ideal balance of structure and flexibility, you'll soon feel resistance to adhering to the schedule requirements. Therefore, think about how the proposed schedule fits your natural rhythm. It takes time to find what kind of work schedule works best. Your preferences will also change over time as your life changes and evolves.

An ideal work schedule should also align with your peak performance hours. *When during the day do you feel most focused and energetic?* Maybe you are most productive in the morning. Or, maybe you feel most inspired in the afternoon. If you plan your periods of focused solo work during your peak performance time, you're more likely to produce quality work with fewer errors and more meaningful impact. It's a practice of Self-Study to understand your own peak performance hours and define your work schedule boundaries.

Just as work environments have become more flexible, work schedules and timing have become more flexible with technology as well. Though technology has helped to make work schedules more flexible, technology has at the same time made work schedules almost obsolete for many people. With technology, e-mail and the ability to stay connected follow us home. *Are we at work or at home?* Offices still represent "work time" but for many, just as much work is done at home. If you have a job that follows you home, boundaries are essential! It may be up to you, not your organization or leader, to set your schedule and boundaries around your work schedule, regardless of location and connectivity.

When evaluating your work schedule, consider social and recreational time. Your time outside of work has an impact on your physical and mental health. Time for recreational activities after work and on weekends, like exercise and time with friends, is almost synonymous with self-care. Movement, ideally in nature away from the screen and work environment, provides short-term and long-term benefits in terms of health and mood. Though solo time for self-care is very important, I have experienced first-hand how regular opportunities to socialize allow you to relax and rejuvenate. We all need time to connect with others in a casual, non-work-related environment.

Finally, what about vacation? The vacation policy should also be such that you can take short or long personal breaks when you need them. Formal time away from work is essential for refueling and rejuvenating. Personal travel always provides new inspiration and energy. Make sure there is regular flexibility and opportunity in your schedule for vacation.

During your interview, ask about schedule requirements and expectations. Compare the expectations with your self-care needs and peak performance hours. Set boundaries around your use of technology. Make sure you will have time for recreation, socializing, and vacation. Now, in my story from the field I'll share my own experience with the elements of possibility.

How I Found Possibility

When it was time to find a full-time job, it was a no-brainer to work for the company where I had interned for two summers. The work aligned with my interests in retail and systems. I fell in love with the environment and the culture. I was in awe of the large, open workspaces with floor-to-ceiling windows. The beautiful community café served healthy food. The office campus was by a river, so I could take walks outside along the water during my breaks to refresh and reset.

The culture of the company was creative and innovative, so I enjoyed this creative energy that I hadn't felt for a long time in engineering school. The environment and the culture, as well as the alignment with my interests, made my job feel full of possibility. I felt inspired and motivated. I looked forward to going to work.

Though the job and the company felt full of possibility, there were aspects of possibility I wasn't aware of when entering the world of full-time work. The first element of possibility that was most challenging for me to navigate was **salary**. It was only after accepting the offer and starting to work that I realized how much I really needed financially to live comfortably. I was used to having the essentials (and more) covered while in school and I wasn't fully aware of my cost of living. I had not answered the questions I prompted in the salary section of this book because I did not have the Awake Apprentice system! So, I had to design my life around the less-than-ideal salary I had accepted.

My lower budget prompted me to cut a lot of my regular spending. *Was the job still possible?* Yes. *Was I doing my best work?* Well, I knew I would have more focus if I didn't have to strategize so much about how to spend and save. Many people face this challenge of adapting to a less-than-ideal salary when they enter the working world.

The salary challenge actually proved to be a good challenge for me because it made me much more aware of my true needs and more grateful for each experience in my life. It woke me up. I took more intentional action to build discipline around my spending habits and consumption. I went through a lot of self-evaluation and practiced Self-Study to understand what I really needed to live well and do my best work. I learned the value of simplicity and actually learned to really enjoy a more minimalist lifestyle, where my space and mind were clearer. I became much smarter and more organized about my spending.

When I was offered a promotion, I entered into negotiations with greater knowledge about the salary I really needed. I realized the importance of the elements of possibility, especially salary, as fuel for my best work and a life outside work. I realized the importance of knowing my true needs and having them covered initially, so that I could have optimal fuel and focus for my work.

My next deep dive into possibility awareness happened when I was offered my second full-time job within that same company. I made a move from the analytics team back to the logistics team to take on a special projects role. With more awareness about my essential elements of possibility, I evaluated my new job opportunity. I was comfortable with the new salary, the schedule, the culture, and the environment. However, I was switching teams and so I would have a new leader and a new team. *How would I know if my new leader would be supportive and offer possibility for me?* Even though the new opportunity aligned with my interests, I didn't know exactly how this new leader and team would affect my day-to-day work.

I soon learned that **leadership** and **culture** are extremely important elements of possibility. My leader in this new role was very wise, transparent, and caring. However, his approach to hiring and cultivating a collaborative environment was not so mindful or effective. A few weeks after I started the job, he recruited a very experienced woman to join the team as my peer. She was much older than I was. She was hired from outside the company and had a very corporate background. She didn't appreciate the creative aspect of the brands and the human side of leadership. Though she had a lot of experience and confidence, she was not a cultural fit for the company and the team. She was hired based on her experience, seniority, and dominant presence; however, her leadership skills and cultural alignment were severely lacking.

Her harsh presence in the office quickly changed the team culture. She would often walk over to my desk, uninvited, and attack me with questions. She often questioned her own team's decision-making before understanding the context and situation fully. At meetings, even with other departments and teams, she raised her voice and gave undue criticism that reflected poorly on our department and company as a whole. Our approaches to leading and working clashed and I immediately felt resistance to working with her on a daily basis. Her team members also felt the burden of negativity, lack of trust, and disrespect. I voiced my concern to my leader (our leader) but he suggested I focus on her potential and make an effort to work with her. So, I did.

For six months, I tried to handle the relationship and the daily situations with poise and equanimity. I worked very objectively with her and did self-care practices to rejuvenate after meetings or interactions with her. I even tried to replenish and realign possibility for myself by limiting my time at work with her. I went to the extent of framing the situation as a positive challenge. I thought that if I approached the situation as something that would make me stronger each day and a better leader, I'd embrace it rather than resist it. Eventually, this approach didn't work anymore. It had gone too far. Her harsh language, negativity, and lack of trust were taking a physical toll on me. I had no energy and no appetite. I no longer looked forward to coming into work; I dreaded it. I spent most of my time at home recovering mentally and emotionally from the long days at work.

Just as I started to lose my sense of motivation and my health, multiple talented people on her team started leaving the company. People on the team were tired and angry. Retention was becoming an issue on a team where operations were essential. I knew something had to be done, since possibility for the team and my own job was severely lacking. I told my leader again about my frustration and the negative impacts she had on the team morale and culture. I explained to him that many people on her team had started to lose motivation and suffered high stress from her leadership. Unfortunately, again, he didn't empathize with my concerns. He largely ignored my call for help. I felt isolated and alone. My well of possibility was drying up quickly. *Without a supportive leader, who had the power to make a change, was there possibility for me in this role and on this team?*

Since I did not have the power to make a change in the departmental structure, I continued to voice my concern at every one-on-one meeting with my leader. I tried to regain his support and my own possibility. I figured that I had nothing to lose at this point. It was known throughout the department that her team and her peers were suffering from her harsh approach to leading and working. Despite my efforts and the voice of others on her team, too, my leader allowed her to continue. People on her team continued to leave and she continued to hire more people that were not cultural fits for the company.

I lost a lot of respect for my leader during this time. The quality of my work and my health suffered. I became depressed when I saw how the culture was changing. A once-happy, motivated team had turned into a mess, full of conflict and disorder. I was in disbelief that the culture had shifted so profoundly within a matter of months. I was upset with myself that I had let it go this far. I was so frustrated. I felt as though I had no control over a desperate situation.

On the outside, everything looked great. I was good at my job and was lucky to work at a beautiful, creative company. On the inside, I felt horrible. **The leadership, the culture, and the people stuff were getting in the way of everything.** I didn't want to give up. I fought for resolution. However, without possibility in the form of support and change from the leadership, I could no longer come to work and contribute. I had lost my health, my motivation, and my inspiration. Even though the work itself aligned with my interest and there were bright moments, it wasn't enough to remedy the lack of possibility.

This was the first time I experienced the profound effect leadership has on team culture and individual possibility. Hiring is a big responsibility and it has huge effects on the team dynamic. It is the responsibility of the top-level leadership to hire the right people and the responsibility of all leaders to listen and work through interpersonal issues. One person can change the collective culture drastically, for better or for worse. It's every person's role to speak up for what is right for the team. It's the leader's duty to listen, understand, respond, and take action.

So, what did I do? It was hard for me to come to terms with letting go of my job at this amazing company. I had spent almost five years of my early career at this company and I really didn't want to leave. The role and the company so closely aligned with my interests. However, without supportive leadership and strong culture, it was impossible to continue my work there. I was so upset with how the situation was handled that I didn't even want to consider another position at the company.

I started a new job search with an elevated understanding about the elements of possibility, especially leadership. This unfortunate and challenging situation had highlighted what was vital for my own possibility. I had new awareness of what possibility conditions to look for in a job. I learned to meditate and reflect on these six elements of possibility.

When interviewing for a new job, I took note of the environment. I inquired about the schedule, the work expectations and opportunities, and, of course, the leadership. Most importantly, I envisioned myself in the new opportunity. I envisioned what opportunity would fuel my fountain of possibility. Finally, after weeks of researching and interviewing, I found a new job opportunity at a new company across the country.

Entering into a job opportunity full of possibility is about knowing yourself and what makes you thrive at work and in life. Equally as important is one's ability to balance patience with action: to see clearly and make a call when it is time to make a change or move on. Moving on is not a loss; it is more often a move in the right direction. Without possibility, there is no future and no growth. We all need our elements of possibility in place in order to be productive, inspired, and connected.

When evaluating jobs for possibility, I found two major challenges. The first is that it was often challenging to find a job that satisfied all of my ideal possibility elements. I realized that this is why it is best to weigh the elements of possibility with each offer you receive. You'll learn how to do this in the exercises. Someday, when you build your own company, you can set up all of your ideal possibility criteria. However, when seeking out a new job, it's often about looking for the best option that satisfies your most important elements of possibility. Also, I realized that our possibility vitals change over time. Just like identifying your interests, identifying if there is possibility for you in a job is a constant practice of self-study as well as assessment of the job conditions. Each person changes over time and so do jobs and organizations. It's essential to reassess and reflect often.

Let's move on to the exercises, where you'll learn to approach and analyze your own elements of possibility.

Possibility

in Action

Possibility Exercises

Without knowing your own needs and your possibility priorities, it's impossible to select a job that will be sustainable and enjoyable. The three possibility exercises will help you to choose jobs that fill your fountain of possibility. They will also inform how you can navigate possibility during your work experience. So many times people accuse their employer or leader of not providing the right support when the person doesn't know what he or she really needs or desires.

The first and second possibility exercises are for identifying your own needs in order to successfully assess your job opportunities. The third possibility exercise is for overcoming possibility obstacles during your work experience. Remember that this is a journey of **Self-Study**!

Exercise 1: Know Thyself

Exercise 2: Assess the Possibility

Exercise 3: Overcome the Obstacles

Supplies:

- Pen or pencil
- Paper
- Journal

Possibility

Exercise 1: Know Thyself

Intention: *Identify your own needs in terms of salary, environment, and schedule to understand your own conditions for possibility at work.*

Let's get really clear about what you need in order to thrive. Take your time to thoughtfully answer the following prompts. If you need more space to expand on your answers, use a journal.

1a. When you reflect on a given month of your life, what products, services, and experiences are most vital to you? List both the things that cost money and the things that do not.

_____

_____

_____

_____

1b. What is the approximate monthly cost of these things? Feel free to make a list and identify each cost.

_____

_____

_____

_____

in Action

Exercise 1: Know Thyself

2. Why are these things so vital to you and how do they support your best self, your energy, and your work?

_____

_____

_____

_____

_____

_____

3. Is there anything that you need to clean out of your living space or budget in order to thrive? What spending habits, activities, or possessions could you let go of?

_____

_____

_____

_____

_____

_____

Possibility

Exercise 1: Know Thyself

4. What is your ideal work environment? What are the qualities of your ideal work environment?

___

___

___

___

5. If you could design your ideal work day, what would your average daily schedule look like and why? Be specific about your starting time, your breaks, the type of work you'd be doing each hour, and your go-home time.

___

___

___

___

Remember that, over time, your answers to these questions will change based on changes in preference and lifestyle. For now, keep your answers to these reflection questions in mind and let's move on to Exercise 2.

Exercise 2: Assess the Possibility

Intention: Chart and assess the elements of possibility in order to to evaluate your job offers and resolve possibility droughts during your work experience.

As an engineer, I love numbers. Well, really I have a love-hate relationship with numbers. Everything cannot be explained with numbers; however, numbers can inform our decision-making and analysis. In this exercise, you will chart and rank the elements of possibility for a given job offer. If you are evaluating multiple offers, this exercise will help you to compare the elements of possibility for each job and give you direction as to which job might be the best apprenticeship for you.

If you feel that possibility is lacking in your current apprenticeship, this exercise will help you identify which elements are lacking and serve as a platform for resolution.

We'll use this ranking chart (example shown in the next page) to rank and then evaluate the elements of possibility in any given job offer.

Turn the page to begin!

Possibility

Exercise 2: Assess the Possibility

Example:

Possibility Element	Importance Rating	My Rating	Element Score
Offer	5	4	20
Salary	3	3	9
Leadership/Team	4	3	12
Environment	4	4	16
Schedule	5	4	20
Culture	3	4	12
Other _____			

Ideal Score **Actual Score** **Total Rating**

120 89 74%

Exercise 2: Assess the Possibility

Filling Out Your Possibility Chart

Step 1. To fill out your ranking chart, begin by placing a number from 1 to 5 in the the first column that represents the level of importance to you. This number should remain constant for all the jobs you evaluate at a given time.

Step 2. In the second column, rank the level of possibility from 1 to 5 for **a specific job offer** that you are evaluating (or for your current job).

Step 3. Multiply across the rows to compute the Element Score and fill out the third column.

Step 4. Compute the Ideal Score by adding up the Importance Ratings and multiplying by 5 (the ideal ranking for all of them).

Step 5. Compute the Actual Score by adding up all of the Element Scores.

Step 6. Compute the Total Rating by dividing the Actual Score by the Ideal Score.

If you have multiple offers, do this chart for each offer based on your knowledge of the elements of possibility. Column 1, Importance Rating, should not change but column 2, my Rating, should change for each job offer. Compare your offer Total Score to assess which job may be best to choose.

If you currently have a job, use this chart to compare each to assess which element scores are lowest and focus on where possibility could improve to fuel your best work.

Possibility

Exercise 2: Assess the Possibility

Your turn!

Possibility Element	Importance Rating	My Rating	Element Score
Offer			
Salary			
Leadership/Team			
Environment			
Schedule			
Culture			
Other _____			

Ideal Score **Actual Score** **Total Rating**

_____ _____ _____

in Action

Exercise 3: Overcome the Obstacles

Intention: *Evaluate your options for refilling the well of possibility at your current job. Feel and think before you act.*

If you realize that you might be in the midst of a possibility drought, what can you do to salvage your support and possibility? Should you stay or should you go? This is what you'll work through in this exercise. This exercise is a great exercise to work through when you find yourself questioning if you have the right possibility at work.

Even the best jobs come with possibility droughts at some point. Sometimes the leadership loses sight of the vision, sometimes the pay is too low, and sometimes a change in the work environment or schedule compromises possibility.

When a possibility drought happens, at first you will likely feel frustrated and disappointed. Your first reaction might be to feel fearful or think about your other options. A common question I receive, when someone I know experiences a possibility drought, is whether they should leave or put up with the lack of possibility.

Remember that in this chapter, we're focusing only on the aspects of possibility, or support needs. In the next chapter, we'll focus on how to gain and sustain potential, or growth opportunities.

Turn the page to begin answering the prompts for Exercise 3.

Possibility

Exercise 3: Overcome the Obstacles

Answer the following prompts. These prompts are a sequential thought flow that will help you work through a possibility drought at work.

1. In general, why do you feel there is a lack of possibility in your current job? Describe the evolution of your experience and <u>identify the key conversations, events, or days when you felt a lack of possibility emerging and why</u>.

_____

_____

_____

_____

_____

2. Based on your answer to question #1, what aspect(s) of possibility (salary, environment, schedule, leadership, or culture) do you feel are lacking the most in your current situation?

_____

_____

_____

in Action

Exercise 3: Overcome the Obstacles

3. If these aspects of possibility from question #2 were in alignment and not lacking at work today, what would that look like? You can think about past experiences or more ideally how this would look day-to-day at work.

_____

_____

_____

_____

_____

_____

4. Who are the people (or person) who have the most influence or control over this aspect(s) of possibility? If it's one person, circle them below. If it's multiple people, circle and rank the options below. If you have identified more than one aspect of possibility in question #2, consider doing this exercise separately for each aspect.

___ Me   ___ Human Resources

___ My leader/boss   ___ Other: _____

___ The leadership/upper management

Possibility

Exercise 3: Overcome the Obstacles

5. Based on your answer to question 4, who would you need help from (to partner with), in order to resolve the possibility drought? How could you start a conversation about questions 1 & 2 and partner with them to find a solution similar to your answer to question 3?

_____

_____

_____

_____

_____

6. How could you provide more possibility for yourself? *Hint: You could commit to partnering with someone you circled in question 4, or think through how you fill your own well in terms of each aspect of possibility.*

_____

_____

_____

_____

_____

in Action

Exercise 3: Overcome the Obstacles

Alright, let's sum this up and get to your action items. More importantly, let's assess your plan for resolution.

7. Based on your answers to the questions so far, do you have an action item for resolving the possibility drought? Do you have a plan to partner with someone or focus on refilling your well of possibility? How? When?

_____

_____

_____

_____

If you found that you can't start a conversation with the person most in control or influential in helping you refill the well of possibility, I encourage you to try anyway. What do you have to lose? I also encourage you to challenge yourself to refill your well of possibility. Sometimes the hardest person to work with is yourself. Think of this challenge as an opportunity to connect with someone new, and to get to know yourself better. This will pay off throughout your career.

If both of these options don't work to ultimately refill the well of possibility in your current job, don't wait too long - your best option for possibility might be to move on to another job. Return to Exercise 2 and evaluate your current job versus other opportunities. I hope that you use these exercises to successfully overcome your obstacles and refill the well of possibility. Make the commitment to reconnect with your interests, as well as your sense of connection, health, and happiness at work.

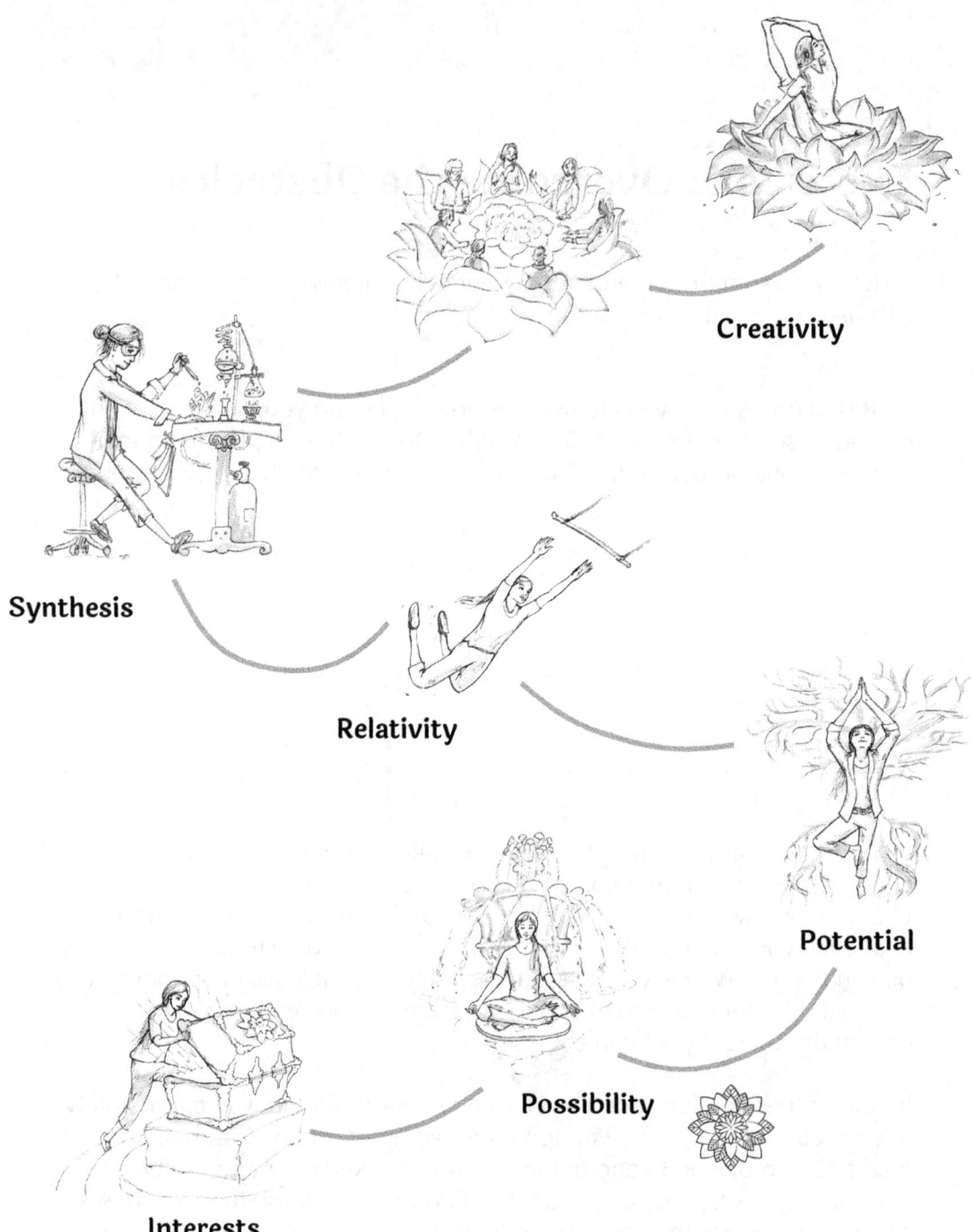

Earth to Creative Leader Tip #2

Investing with Intention

In this chapter, we talked about how to determine the salary you need in order to feel your best and to find success in your job. Awake Apprentices do not choose a job based on the money alone; they lead with their interests. However, sometimes a salary fuels possibility beyond your basic financial needs. **Excess money can cause harm if you don't think about how to spend your disposable income with intention.** If you make more than you need for you day-to-day expenses, how should you spend or invest your money? Here are **four ways to invest your extra money.**

Experiences and Opportunities that will Fuel your Possibility: Signing up for a weekly yoga class, a community club, or buying organic produce can add immense value to your work and your life. You'll be surprised how supplying your own fountain with support can fuel your best work.

Learning Experiences: As we'll talk about in the next chapter, investing in your potential by expanding your skills and knowledge is always a great investment. Sign up for a class that aligns with your interests or provides an opportunity to practice creativity. This is a great way to spend weekends.

Visiting Friends: No matter how busy you are as an apprentice, keeping like-minded friends that also provide support is essential.

Future Creative Endeavors: By saving a little bit each month during my early career, I was able to fully invest in my creative endeavors when I was ready. I am thankful to my younger self for having this instinct and vision.

Up Next...

Let's now dive into **Chapter 3, Potential**, which is all about how to reach your potential at work with learning and development opportunities.

Chapter 3
Potential

Fuel Your Potential

After leading with your interests and finding a job that offers possibility, the next important phase of the Awake Apprentice journey is unlocking your potential. Potential is the heart of what makes a regular job into an invaluable experience of applied learning. A job that fuels your potential provides continuous opportunities for learning and development.

Awake Apprentices are life-long learners, so they are always seeking to learn more and expand their realm of awareness and set of capabilities. Just as a tree extends its branches, Awake Apprentices seek out opportunities to extend their skills and knowledge past their current realm.

Potential is a key aspect of an Awake Apprentice's journey because applying new learnings in action is the vehicle for discovering your unique skills and strengths, as well as your unique purpose. **As you expand your skills and knowledge through real-world experience, you also strengthen your abilities and awareness.** Your branches expand with new knowledge and capabilities and your roots grow stronger with greater awareness of what you want to contribute and who you want to be.

Potential opportunities allow you to grow and prepare you for the next step in your career. By continuously growing your skill set, knowledge base, and realm of experience, you'll be prepared for a promotion when the time is right. By proactively seeking out learning and development opportunities, you will take control of your own career path and the pace of your advancement.

For a job to serve as an apprenticeship, it must provide continuous learning and development opportunities that expand your potential. When we begin in a new role, there are plenty of learning and development opportunities. The job itself presents an opportunity to learn something new. Learning how to master the job is a development process. However, when you start asking, *"What's next from here? What else is there to learn and*

A job that fuels your potential provides continuous opportunities for learning and development.

do? What other connections can I make?", then you're ready for new potential. Awake Apprentices don't want to be stuck on a hamster-wheel of sameness after three months in a new job. **Potential opportunities keep a job fresh, inspiring, and challenging, even when some aspects of the job become tedious or easy.** Let's take a closer look at what potential opportunities at work really look like and how to embark on new opportunities for personal and professional development.

◆ ◆ ◆

How can you find potential opportunities at work?

Potential opportunities come in many forms. When evaluating a job, it is important to consider what you will learn and how the experience will push you past your comfort zone. Beyond the basic job responsibilities, there are ways to facilitate learning and development experiences to keep growing. Any experience that expands your knowledge, skills, or awareness serves as an opportunity to expand your potential.

Potential could come in the form of a special project, expanded responsibility, or a leadership opportunity. Sometimes these opportunities are prompted by your leader and sometimes you have to seek them out yourself. Now, we'll take a closer look at five specific ways to expand your potential at work.

Opportunity 1: Special Projects

A special project is a short-term assignment that allows you to learn and develop your skills while delivering value to the team and organization. **Special projects have both functional outcomes for the team as well as learning outcomes for the project leader** (the Awake Apprentice). For example, the topic of a special project could be to improve an old process, develop a new tool, or advise on strategic direction. In terms of the timeline, special projects usually last anywhere from two to six months.

Before starting a special project, there should be specific learning objectives and a specific goal for the project. A special project often involves entering uncharted territory to fix an unresolved issue or lead a new development initiative. Though special projects most often offer opportunities to develop your technical skills, special projects also provide an opportunity to manage a project from start to finish. Designing a project, planning how you'll execute, and following through are important skills to master as an Awake Apprentice. Special projects are often cross-functional, and they provide an opportunity to connect with new people from different parts of the organization or even outside the organization.

Ideally, your leader will offer you special projects from time to time to keep the work fresh and exciting, and to give you an opportunity to develop new skills and practice your project leadership. However, you should not wait for an invitation; if you spot an opportunity to improve a process or develop a tool that will add value, suggest it to your leader.

Before working on a special project, make sure to run it by your leader. Work alongside them while designing the project to make sure it's value-adding for the team. Make sure your leader is aligned and that he or she is supportive of the way you plan to use your time at work.

Opportunity 2: Learning Experiences

While special projects are periodic assignments with a specific objective, it's also important to build your skill set and knowledge base through formal learning. Learning experiences are opportunities to gain exposure to new concepts, tools, and knowledge that will improve your work and future potential.

At work, the most meaningful learning often happens with your leader. In one-on-one meetings, ask to spend time with your leader learning a skill or talking about something that will expand your knowledge base. It's best to plan ahead and prepare questions. Questions facilitate discussion and prompt new information. Ask for his or her opinion on something you're working on. Ask for a demo. **Your leader is often the most valuable source of wisdom.** Transferring knowledge is also a great way to build a stronger bond with your leader.

You can facilitate learning opportunities for yourself at the office by asking for opportunities to practice skills you want to develop. The office environment provides applied learning opportunities to develop new capabilities and strengths. For example, if presenting or public speaking is a challenge for you, ask for an opportunity to lead a meeting. You can even ask to set up your own meeting to practice presenting information to new team members or to present your current work challenges and learnings to your leader. Give yourself more than one shot; ask your leader or leadership for continuous opportunities to practice your challenge areas in action. Learning experiences help to overcome weaknesses and to overcome fears in the way of your potential, especially in business.

All learning does not happen at work. It's sometimes necessary to escape from the office environment in order to take a course or training. Courses and trainings are a great way to remove yourself from the day-to-day work in order to focus solely on learning. You'll bring back fresh ideas and perspective when you remove yourself from the work environment and mindset to explore and learn. For example, you might need to take a course to learn new software because in a future project or role you'll need to know how to use the software. If you identify a skill or capability that you need to learn off-site at a professional learning center or school, suggest it to your leader.

Sometimes, you might need to pursue your own learning opportunities outside of work while you wait for a potential opportunity at work. **Always invest in your own learning and don't wait for an invitation!** It's awesome if your leader proposes learning opportunities for you; however, if that is not the case, you cannot afford to wait around. Take charge of your own learning experiences and forge your own path. Whether it's as simple as reading a new book or as big as attending a conference or course, invest in your own potential and never stop learning. Make it a goal to learn something new every week no matter how small. Record your new learnings in a journal each week to celebrate new learning wins and reflect on what you should aim to learn next.

Opportunity 3: Immersions

An immersion is an opportunity to shadow someone on your team or to work with another team for a period of time. **Spending a day in someone else's shoes, or shadowing someone else's work, provides an opportunity to learn new skills and gain perspective.**

Shadowing others on the team often expedites the onboarding process when starting a new job. Immersions with people on other teams provide even more context for how the work you do relates to the organization as a whole and benefits others within the organization.

Shadowing and immersing yourself in a different team's approach to work can also give you new ideas for how to approach your work and, in the future, your own creative endeavor. Working in a silo, on your own, quickly turns into mundane, hamster-wheel-like activity. By spending time with someone else and shadowing how they approach their work, you will gain new ideas for how to approach your own.

Through immersion experiences, you often learn new skills and new ways of doing things that you would not have come up with on your own.

There is also energy exchanged while spending time with someone else, especially when they also want to learn from you and exchange ideas for how to work more efficiently or with more ease. After an immersion experience, you'll often return to your work with new ideas and appreciation. Even higher-level leaders benefit from shadowing other departments to learn how others work and to share ideas for best practices.

Finally, immersion experiences also provide new perspective and help cultivate greater empathy. If you work cross-functionally, meaning you often work with another team on tasks or projects, an immersion with that team will give you understanding of what another team goes through day-to-day. Video calls or conversations in meetings often don't provide enough context to really understand the challenges another person or team experiences. Direct experience provides real perspective and will supercharge your ability to collaborate.

Opportunity 4: Promotion or New Responsibility

When you receive an opportunity to take on new responsibility, you are prompted to learn how to adapt and reprioritize. Many talented Awake Apprentices fear taking on new responsibility because they feel that it will compromise their current workload. Some people feel that taking on new responsibility should always come along with a promotion. However, when viewed as an opportunity to learn and prepare for the next level, expanded responsibility becomes a potential opportunity and a gift. Expanding your workload challenges you to spread your wings. Learning how to prioritize and adapt to new working conditions is essential for building strength and versatility!

Expanded responsibility is often prompted by your leader. It most often means adding new tasks and responsibilities to your regular schedule. If you're ready to take more on your plate, ask for or be open to taking on more responsibility. **Expanded responsibility should not feel like a burden but instead it should feel like an opportunity to learn and grow.** If you're feeling a bit stagnant in your day-to-day work and have mastered your current work scope, talk to your leader and offer to take on more responsibility.

It's true that more responsibility usually involves a promotion. A promotion seems like it is always a good thing. It is something most people work toward and reach for after mastering a new job. However, sometimes your responsibility will be expanded without a promotion. *Is that fair? When it is right to seek or ask for a promotion?* A promotion most often means three things: more responsibility, a new title, and higher payment. These three things are related. I would argue that a promotion is not really a promotion (or shouldn't be) without all three of these things happening at or around the same time. A promotion involves higher payment because you are expanding the earning potential for the organization. However, don't hesitate to take on more responsibility if it fuels your potential and prepares you for the next level (and the promotion that you crave).

Remember that potential is all about learning to explore your own capabilities while expanding the potential of the team and the organization as well. Referring back to possibility, it's important that you have enough energy, enough support, and enough resources to take on a larger workload. More output sometimes requires more input. Find what that form of input is for you, whether that input is more focused solo time, more financial support, or a different work environment in order to succeed in expanding your potential.

Opportunity 5: Leadership Experience

Leading a team, whether one person or 100 people, is an opportunity to learn about working with people. Leading is maybe the most rewarding learning experience that offers endless challenges, insights, and growth opportunities. The desire to be a manager or leader should come from a desire to guide an initiative and team of people forward. It should come from the desire to be a mentor and expand the team's potential, individually and collectively. Leading a team prompts you to enhance your communication and organizational skills. More importantly, leading a team prompts you to learn how to manage people and motivate people.

As we talked about in the previous chapter, a leader largely determines the possibility for their team members. It's important to understand how to provide potential for others. This is learned by experiencing potential opportunities yourself. So, before leading others, it's important to do the self work in knowing what fuels your own potential. Leaders that cut corners and secure promotions without really doing the work to grow and develop real skills quickly become insecure and lose respect from their own team. The only way is to develop skills through your own potential opportunities. This experience will give you a real-world skill set and you will learn how to provide potential opportunities for others, too. While other aspects of work can become tedious or mundane, leadership is an ever-evolving and very exciting aspect of working in an organization.

Mentorship is a huge aspect of leading others and facilitating potential opportunities. As a leader, you will learn to be a mentor and a guide. Mentors are like teachers, but they work alongside the mentee in a similar line of work. A mentor, or leader, is just a bit further down the path. Every job is different and though most team members will start with certain skills and knowledge, they'll likely need an infusion of knowledge and time with you in order to get up to speed. Leaders must enjoy working with people and seeing people grow and evolve. **While leading, you will learn to make regular time in your schedule for teaching and helping others.** You will learn how to be an active guide and a mirror for others along their path.

Leading also prompts us to take a new level of ownership. In order to motivate people, it's important to work in alignment with your interests and to be dedicated to the mission. When the leader is not working in alignment with his or her interests, it becomes obvious to team members and dedication declines. When team members complain or vent, it's often because they need to reconnect to the higher mission and value of their work. This means you, as the leader, need to provide that higher-level perspective and motivation.

Before taking a leadership position, make sure you're working in alignment with a mission that speaks to your interests. The path is all connected. There are so many ways to fuel your potential and continuously learn when you approach a job as an apprenticeship. As you'll see in my story, a diverse collection of learning experiences is essential for cultivating independence and discovering your purpose.

All of these potential opportunities are ways to expand your branches and deepen your roots. **Work experience in an organization provides an ideal platform for experiences of applied learning.** Without taking on new experiences and responsibilities, it is impossible to know where you want to go and what you're meant to do. Potential is the essential part of a job that makes it a true apprenticeship. Awake Apprentices never stop learning! In my story, I'll explain how I found potential opportunities and used them to fuel my progress.

From Learning to Leading

Potential opportunities at work serve as experiences of applied learning that allow us to develop new skills and deeper understanding. When I entered the corporate world of retail as an intern, I didn't think work and learning happened simultaneously. I thought that you go to work to simply apply your skills. School is for learning. Work is for working. I realized the importance of personal evolution and experiences of applied learning while working with my first leader.

As a new intern, with no previous work experience in retail or supply chain, I quickly realized that I needed guidance and specific training to actually be useful at work. School had prepared me in terms of professional etiquette and organization, but I lacked the industry knowledge and analytical skill set that I needed to do my new job well. I still had a lot to learn on the job!

During the first week at my new job, my leader walked me through the work he had planned for me to do that summer. I was somewhat overwhelmed by the amount of new information and tools I would need to learn in order to accomplish the work. Luckily, my leader realized that even though I was brand new, I had the interest, dedication, and ability to learn quickly. He was a great teacher and a patient mentor. Even though he was a director of a large department and had a lot to do, he still directly invested in my development and success. I remember sitting with him for almost an hour each day during my first month of work as he transferred knowledge and demonstrated how to work the systems I needed to know in order to do my work. His knowledge about how to work the systems, dig into the details, and spend time and attention impressed me and he immediately earned my respect.

I didn't realize until later on in my career how fortunate I was to have a leader that not only taught me the skills I needed to do my job well, but also provided potential opportunities to continue to develop my skills and knowledge. He provided mentoring sessions, special projects, and immersions so that I could improve and grow. He spent time in one-on-one meetings teaching me the tools and industry knowledge I needed to succeed in my work that summer and beyond. He took our team on immersions to the stores and to our supply chain partners to shadow and learn the greater context of our operations.

Soon, with my new skills and knowledge, I was able to work more independently. The ongoing tasks I was responsible for became easier and I became more confident. My leader was able to delegate work to me more efficiently and I could execute more effectively. In just two months, I had learned a whole new set of tools and realm of real-world knowledge. **His dedication to my growth fueled my interest in the company and deepened my dedication to the team.**

After I had mastered the skills I needed to be an analyst, my leader then gave me special projects that involved research and cross-functional work with other teams. He challenged me to extend my capabilities and knowledge. The special projects ranged from industry research, to small ad-hoc analyses, to helping him prepare for a meeting. It wasn't always easy and I often had to ask for help. However, these special projects pushed me beyond my comfort zone and prompted me to work cross-functionally with others on the team and other departments to succeed. There were layers of applied learning experiences within each special project that helped me to become more skilled, collaborative, and curious.

This first job experience gave me a healthy appetite for learning on the job. When I had opportunities to learn and expand my potential, I felt inspired and abundant. I felt useful and as though I was contributing to something that aligned with my interests and desired impacts.

After almost two years in this position, I suddenly felt stagnant for the first time. I craved new learning opportunities. I even started to feel a bit frustrated. I realized that I needed to talk with my leader and ask for new opportunities to learn. He listened to my concerns and we had a good discussion about my desire to grow and take on more responsibility. However, there wasn't an opportunity to take on more responsibility or move into a new position at that time on our team. I continued to feel as though I was learning redundant information and using the same skills over and over. I was eager to grow, explore new territory, and learn more. So, I took matters into my own hands. I started to schedule my own shadow immersions with other people on the team when I had open time. This was a great way to bond with others on the team, learn about the holistic workings of the team, and gain perspective.

A few months later, I realized that I was really ready to graduate to a new role. I put out my feelers for new opportunities within the organization. I soon found a full-time job on a different team with a new leader. The job was perfect for me because I would use all my analytical skills I had built over the previous two years, but apply the skills in a new realm of the company. It was time for a fresh start where I could continue to build my potential.

Finding a leader who is dedicated to developing your potential in order to strengthen the team and help you progress is essential for Awake Apprentices. **A great leader provides potential opportunities including mentoring, immersion opportunities, special projects, and expanded responsibility. However, it's also important to take your career development and personal growth journey upon yourself, as well.** Only you know when it's time for a change and a new opportunity to grow and evolve. Ask your leader for support but take ownership of your path.

When I became a leader of a small team almost three years after starting that first internship, my leadership style reflected much of my first leader's approach. This mentorial leadership style always remained important to me as a way to invest in people development, cultivate connection amongst the team and retain talented team members.

Always seek out potential opportunities for yourself and, as a leader, give potential opportunities to others. This is the key to individual and collective growth.

Potential

in Action

Potential Exercises

The three exercises in this section will prompt you to think about your professional development goals, make a plan for growth at work, and think about how you can take control of your own development outside of work as well.

It might be tempting to read through the exercises only, but know that these exercises are only effective if you actually work through them. <u>Write down your answers</u>!

Exercise 1: Set Your Growth Goals

Exercise 2: Propose a Plan

Exercise 3: Opportunities Outside of Work

Supplies:

- Pen or pencil
- Paper
- Journal

Potential

Exercise 1: Set Your Growth Goals

Intention: *Brainstorm your goals and intentions to set the direction for your professional and personal growth.*

Though some leaders or influencers tell us how we should grow and what we should learn, sustainable and meaningful development happens when we intentionally choose the direction ourselves. Use this exercise to reflect on your work experience and your interests to set the direction and goals for your learning and growth. Answer the prompts. If you need more space, use a separate journal.

1. Your strengths are your <u>inherent</u> skills and qualities that add value and make you unique. When you reflect on your work experience (and maybe school, too), what would you say are your **strengths**? What strengths are inherent to your personality and work style? List 4 or 5 of your strengths.

_____

_____

_____

_____

_____

_____

in Action

Exercise 1: Set Your Growth Goals

2. **Why** did you choose the strengths that you listed in question #1? Write down the situations or reasons that you identified these strengths. Think about how your strengths have been applied and proven in action.

_____
_____
_____
_____
_____
_____
_____

3. What are your core **skills** or capabilities? What are skills you use at work and in life that you have learned and mastered? List at least 3 of your skills.

_____
_____
_____
_____
_____
_____
_____

Potential

Exercise 1: Set Your Growth Goals

4. What **experiences** have shaped your professional growth the most? If you were to tell two or three stories from your work experience that were most pivotal in your professional and personal growth, what stories would you tell? Briefly document them here and continue in your journal.

in Action

Exercise 1: Set Your Growth Goals

5. Reflecting on your interests from Chapter 1 and impactful experiences from question #4, set 3 **learning and growth objectives**. If you could learn more about something, or progress in some way personally and/or professionally, what 3 goals would you set for yourself?

_____

_____

_____

_____

_____

6. Which of your strengths and skills do you **already have** that align with these goals? What strengths and skills do you **need to develop** in order move toward these goals?

_____

_____

_____

_____

_____

Potential

Exercise 2: Pitch the Potential

***Intention**: Brainstorm and clearly articulate the value of a special project in order to learn something new and contribute something of value. Deepen your experience of applied learning!*

Now that you are more aware of your own strengths, skills, and learning goals, you're ready to brainstorm and draft a special project plan for a potential opportunity. A special project plan is a concise and powerful way to pitch an idea. There are many ways and many variations of special projects, but the basic essence of any special project is to work on a specific focused solo project for a short duration (ranging from 2 to 6 months) in order to contribute something of value and learn along the way.

Many apprentices ask for or pitch ideas without doing the work of really evaluating the opportunity and the value, both for them as a learning experience and for the team or organization. This exercise is profound because in the process of writing the pitch, you will justify the learning and contribution value of a potential opportunity. It's important to think through the importance of a project and the intention behind it before spending time discussing it and working on it. Intention and vision are key! The result is a project plan that you can use in pitching the opportunity to your leader, if you need his or her approval.

Let's begin...

in Action

Exercise 2: Pitch the Potential

Before writing your special project plan, it's a good practice to brainstorm ideas for special projects you'd like to work on and pitch. Use the space below to brainstorm special project ideas that you'd like to work on. Refer to your interests from Chapter 1, as well as your strengths and growth goals from Exercise 1.

_____

_____

_____

_____

_____

_____

_____

_____

Turn the page to review an example of a special project plan and the breakdown of the components before drafting your own.

Potential

Special Project Outline Example

Opportunity Name: Competitive Research - Pricing Model

Intention/Mission: To compare alternative pricing models, learn how different companies approach trip pricing for customers and partners, and improve our own.

Objective: To develop our own approach that optimizes price for the customer, partners, and our margin.

Learning Goal(s): Comparative research, model building, and presenting

Value-add(s): Improve our customer and partner relationships, new customer acquisition, increase margin and profit for R&D

Major Steps: Research, organize information, build model, make presentation, and propose implementation plan

Timeline: Three weeks

in Action

Exercise 2: Pitch the Potential

Here is quick description of the components of the special project plan. Review these along with the example on the opposite page. Then, turn the page to draft your own!

Opportunity Name: Name the project or opportunity you're proposing.

Intention: In what new *direction* do you hope this will move the team?

Objective: What is the concrete objective or projected *outcome* of the work involved?

Learning Goal(s): What do you hope to *learn* in the process?

Value-add(s): What specific *value* will this work add to the team and organization?

Major Steps: What work or specific action is involved at a high level?

Timeline: How much time do you estimate the project or opportunity will take?

Tip: Though a project plan largely speaks for itself, it's best to schedule an in-person meeting with the person (or people) you need approval from to work on your project. This process also comes in handy for pitching learning experiences like a conference, side project, or learning course.

Potential

Exercise 2: Pitch the Potential

Your turn!

       Opportunity Name: _____

       Intention: _____

       Objective: _____

       Learning Goal(s): _____

       Value-add(s): _____

       Major Steps: _____

       Timeline: _____

in Action

Exercise 3: Grow Outside of Work

Intention: *Take matters into your own hands and fuel your development outside of work to move toward your potential.*

Sometimes, during flat or stagnant periods at work, it's necessary to fuel your own potential outside of your job. This should not be the norm - you should have opportunities for growth at work to learn and move toward your potential. However, sometimes you have to take matters into your own hands when work potential is flat.

Try one or more of these suggestions when you need to fuel your own potential. Turn the page to begin!

Potential

Exercise 3: Grow Outside of Work

- **Read Books**: Reading an inspiring and functional book provides new motivation and inspiration. Secondly, reading a book helps to build new skills and gain new perspective. Start your book search at your local book store, online, or by asking friends and peers for recommendations. Make sure you're excited about reading the book and make sure it sparks your curiosity.

- **Take Courses**: Taking a course in person or online is a great opportunity to learn something new on your own. I find that the best way to learn is in person. Take a course or set of classes that is long enough (4-10 weeks of consistent study) to really immerse in the material.

- **Launch a Side Project**: Launch your own side project, alone or with friends. Work on it in the morning, evening, and on weekends. Return to your interests or invest in a new interest that sparks your curiosity and connection. Use the Project Plan outline to design your project.

- **Schedule Coffee Chats**: Use your open time at work to schedule coffee breaks with peers and team members. Conversations with different people offer great opportunities to learn and exchange ideas. Keep the conversation positive!

- **Take Interviews**: An interview might seem like a waste of time if you're not serious about leaving your job, but interviews are actually awesome learning opportunities. Go for an interview at a different company to brush up your interviewing skills, learn how other companies operate, and evaluate your current professional potential.

- **Contribute to Publications and Podcasts**: Find a professional publication or podcast to contribute to. Write an article or share your ideas on a public platform. This is great public writing or speaking practice, and content to add to your resume!

Exercise 3: Grow Outside of Work

- **Focus on Health**: During busy or stressful work periods, we often neglect our health. When you have a flat or stagnant period at work, this is the perfect time to focus on your health. Take the time to cook a new recipe at home, make time for exercise, and get plenty of sleep! All of these health-related efforts will also help to reduce stress and fuel your energy.

- **Practice Constructive Rest**: In my first guidebook, *Awake Leadership*, I talk about how Constructive Rest is rest that is functional - in that it fuels your best work. Find your favorite ways of practicing Constructive Rest. For example, you could take a bath, practice yoga or meditation, or watch an inspiring movie.

- **Time with Friends and Family**: We should always make time for friends and family, but slower periods of work make for an even better opportunity to reconnect with special people we don't see or talk with everyday during busy work times. Schedule a call or meet-up with a friend or family member to catch up.

- **Update Professional Profiles**: How outdated is your resume? How outdated is your LinkedIn profile? Take time to reflect on your professional progress and update your professional profiles.

- **Get organized**: This is so important! The whirlwind of work often leaves our physical workspace, digital workspace, and our homes in a chaotic unorganized mess. In my second guidebook, *Awake Ethics*, I talk about a cleaning and organizing exercise called Soji. Practice Soji by taking 20 minutes per day to organize your physical and digital workspaces. Do the same at home. You'll notice how your focus and efficiency improves when you have a clean space and can more easily access your resources.

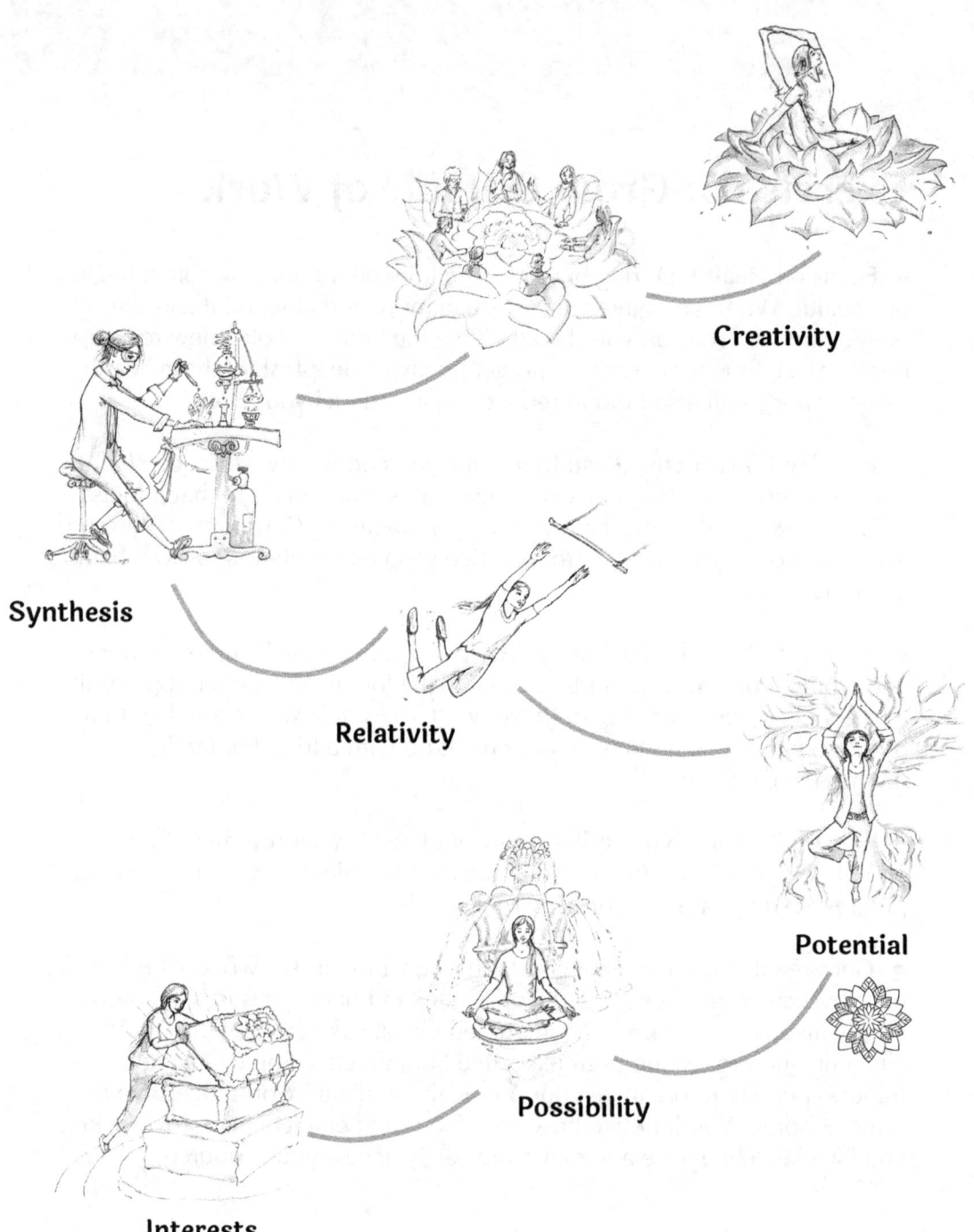

Earth to Creative Leader Tip #3

Fuel the Potential of Others

This tip is about giving in order to receive… or giving in order to make the world a better place. Busy people rarely pause to think about how they are fueling the potential of others around them. Especially in the business world, it's easy to get caught up in our own progress. However, your success is probably thanks to others as well – a leader, mentor, or connection – who have helped you to move forward and who have given you positive motivation.

Most workplaces lack positive acknowledgement and support amongst co-workers. As an Awake Apprentice, think about how you can fuel the potential of others around you. For example, if you are a leader of a team, you can use the guidance in this chapter to provide opportunities for your team members.

Whether you are a leader of a team or an individual contributor, you can still provide opportunities for others around you. Maybe it's as simple as positively acknowledging someone who went beyond expectations. Maybe it's providing a positive reference or review for someone else. Maybe it's connecting two people who may benefit from meeting each other because they have similar interests or goals.

Wouldn't it be nice if others cared about your potential and helped you to advance each day? Once you start to provide potential for other people, you'll realize others will do the same for you. Lead by example in building a team of connected, mindful apprentices that fuel each other's potential.

Up Next…

Next is **Chapter 4, Relativity**, where you'll learn ways to gather new and different experiences. Prepare to explore unknown territory and venture outside your comfort zone! Let's go.

Chapter 4

Relativity

Experience Relativity

Now, we move onward and upward to experience Relativity! Relativity involves embarking on new experiences beyond your current job and venturing outside your comfort zone, such as taking a new job or living in a different country. **Relativity displaces you physically and mentally in order to see through new eyes, from a new perspective.**

Relativity is powerful because it involves displacement; moving from your current location to another. Displacement is often perceived as a negative word; however, in a career, displacement is a gift. I believe the most profound relativity we experience is when we are displaced the most. Displacement helps us to find our true center. By wobbling around our center and getting pulled away from our center, we learn our true center. When you experience relativity, you learn what you like and what you don't like. You see yourself and the world through new eyes.

For Awake Apprentices, the most powerful experience of relativity is to take on a new job. Relativity can also happen through smaller changes and experiences like a summer internship or a trip around the world to volunteer. An experience of relativity gives you an opportunity to expand your awareness by taking on a new role, in a new place, with new challenges. Though change is challenging, it helps build strength and gain broader perspective.

With each experience of relativity, you'll experiment with going away from your current comfort zone in order to adapt to new conditions. You can only learn your ideal environment, culture, and schedule through experiencing different options. Relativity allows you to learn more about yourself by experiencing life through a new lens, under different circumstances. Relativity provides perspective, even beyond what you can imagine, about your career purpose and goals.

We each find our own center through deeper self-awareness but also through seeing how we fit in to contribute in different ways. We take the leap to try on different careers and cultures and

To come up with new ideas that are functional and creative, we need inspiration and a broad range of perspectives.

eventually choose the best fit or create our own.

Ultimately, relativity is essential for Awake Apprentices because relativity is a vehicle for developing solutions and new creations. To come up with new ideas that are functional and creative, you need inspiration and a broad range of perspectives. Big changes and new experiences bring on awakenings and transformational ideas! Relativity is an essential phase for creating original solutions and new offerings.

Relativity is not an act of escaping but an act of expansion and growth. Relativity most often happens because your interests, possibility, or potential at your current apprenticeship are lacking. Sometimes, it happens because a new opportunity arises naturally. Whatever the reason for the transition, Awake Apprentices always make a transition to a better state. Reach higher. Return to your interests, possibility needs, and potential desires to select your next apprenticeship.

A relativity experience can radically change the direction of your career path and guide you further toward your unique purpose. In this chapter, we'll discuss the benefits of relativity, how and when to choose a new apprenticeship, and how to navigate transitions. If you are considering making a move to a new job or taking a leap of faith, I hope that this chapter provides some inspiration and guidance.

The Promises of Relativity

When you navigate relativity experiences with awareness and intention, the benefits are invaluable. The transition of letting go of your current job in order to pursue and acclimate to a new job is often the most challenging part. However, transitions teach us a lot about ourselves and prepare us for the future. **Once you make the leap and land in your new job, the immersive fresh experience often sparks new awakenings and insights about yourself and about the world.** Here are five promises of relativity experiences to guide and inspire you as you consider reaching for something new.

Promise 1: Self-Awareness

Self-awareness is about knowing your strengths, tendencies, and purpose. When someone works too long in a single role or environment, they develop a perception of themselves that is greatly influenced by their immediate context and circumstances. They believe that they are good (and maybe the best) at certain things even though they have been working in a very specific, siloed environment. They see themselves and the world through a single lens.

There is nothing wrong with honing your strengths in the same field or company; however, in order to develop deeper self-awareness and discover your unique creative potential, it's essential to shift roles and environments. It's impossible to know your innate strengths without jumping into the unknown and putting your strengths and abilities to the test under different conditions.

When you experience relativity, your innate strengths emerge. The parts of yourself that were conditioned and characteristic of your old context (but not yourself) fade away. **Relativity experiences awaken deeper self-awareness and highlight your inherent strengths that are truly our innate strengths, independent of your conditions.**

The Awake Apprentice journey is a path of developing self-awareness. You will never be able to see yourself, or experience yourself completely in a vacuum, void of environmental or situational realities. However, relativity allows you to learn more about your inherent power by working in different situations and environments in order to become even more powerful and authentically yourself. Instead of framing a transition as a negative struggle, it's important to see it as an opportunity to learn more about yourself, your elements of possibility, and your potential.

Promise 2: Confidence

With newfound self-awareness comes newfound confidence. When faced with a decision or challenge that involves risk, most people give up or opt out in favor of the norm. Many people never take a leap for a new experience because they fear failure or they fear that change will disrupt their comfortable norm.

Embarking on an experience of relativity is a leap of faith. You don't know exactly how your new job or opportunity will unfold. However, relativity always presents an opportunity to move forward and emerge stronger in the face of uncertainty.

When you jump into the unknown with intention and enthusiasm, you are more likely to succeed. It always helps to set your intention. Setting an intention for your leap of faith gives you a vision for what lies on the other side. If you can't build the self-confidence to take small and large leaps with positivity and hope, you'll never move forward. **The only way to succeed is by trusting yourself, as well as connecting to your intention and your intuition.**

Relativity is a vehicle for building confidence. As you build self-awareness and confidence through relativity experiences, you'll find that you also become a better leader at work and in life. Taking the lead of your life involves intention, dedication, and follow through. To be a great leader of others and lead by example, one must have bravery and a strong internal compass.

These characteristics are only developed through experience on your own Awake Apprentice journey.

Promise 3: Empathy

The world is interconnected. Humans are independent yet interconnected. As an Awake Apprentice, it is your mission to figure out how you fit into the larger picture in order to contribute toward a greater collective world. One of the best ways to learn and discover where you fit into the larger picture is by working with others toward a common mission or goal.

Building relationships and seeing how you fit into the greater whole is a vital aspect of working with a team and advancing as an Awake Apprentice. When you start a new job, one of the most important onboarding activities is to observe and get to know the people you are working with. **New job experiences often start as an anthropology exercise in observing your peers and how they operate.**

Though it can be difficult to learn a new way of working and how to work with a new team of people, this challenge will keep you on your toes and raise your sense of awareness about yourself and others. When you take the time to understand other people's approach and needs, you'll naturally pay more attention, respond more thoughtfully, and pick up cues about how to act and acclimate in new situations.

People in a different organization or environment will have different backgrounds and cultural norms. As you observe and work with people with different backgrounds and ways of working, you'll develop greater empathy. **Empathy is the ability to relate to and even share the feelings of another person.** As Awake Apprentices, empathy is essential for coming up with solutions and creations that serve a purpose for others. You always have an opportunity to develop empathy, but relativity especially raises this awareness and provides a fresh platform for collaboration. Relativity helps strengthen your understanding, acceptance, and appreciation for others.

Developing relationships with different kinds of people through a shared environment, circumstances, and mission will also prompt you to break down your barriers and drop your ego. Your perception about what is normal or right might even come into question. You must reflect on your actions and values in order to develop your own voice and lead by example. Relativity experiences provide a way to refine your perspective and discover your true values and purpose for others.

Promise 4: Solutions and New Ideas

So far, we have talked about three promises of relativity. The three that I have talked about so far are deep, internal promises that prepare you for manifesting your creative potential. Relativity experiences also give you inspiration for how to share your innate strengths, skills, and creative purpose with the world. Experiences of relativity don't just change you internally; they help to discover how you want to share your creative potential with the world.

With each new job, you'll learn new ways of solving problems that you hadn't been exposed to before. You'll learn new techniques from each person you encounter. Eventually, you'll develop your own tool belt and knowledge of universal problems that need your solutions. A wider realm of experiences allows you to practice decision-making and problem solving in choosing how to apply your skills to new tasks and challenges.

When you embrace a completely new function, environment, and schedule, you'll also awaken latent energy and focus. Have you ever found that trying something new, or doing something familiar in a different environment is tiring but invigorating at the same time? This new challenge prompts you to practice greater awareness and build new strength. **Fresh energy and sharper attention enable us to be better problem solvers, soak in new inspiration, and come up with big ideas.**

Learning from others and sharpening your attention are important steps toward becoming innovative. When you see something familiar done in a new or different way, this often reveals a missing piece in your formerly-unsolvable puzzles. Relativity experiences spark new ideas about how to approach problems and create new value in the world.

As you observe differences and similarities between companies, you can observe trends in what problems arise over and over again. These problems that follow you from day-to-day or from job-to-job are begging to be solved... maybe solved by you! As you'll see in the next chapter, a collection of different experiences can bring about realizations about the world and ideas for solutions.

Promise 5: Freedom

Freedom is the ability to choose how to spend your time and where to place your awareness. Through experiences of relativity, you'll learn more about what your version of freedom truly is in this lifetime. You'll learn more about our interests and how to follow your interests through work experience.

Relativity allows you to experience different schedules, environments, and cultures that give you clues as to what your version of freedom really is. With a collection of different versions of what your reality can be, you can pick and choose what will make up your true version of Freedom in order to discover your purpose and design your life. In order to find your purpose, freedom is often a necessary ingredient. By discovering your purpose, you will find more freedom.

Some people are more open to change than others. People who easily embrace change find a sense of freedom in the ability to move and not attach to a certain place or identity. On the other hand, people that are change-averse have different reasons for resisting or avoiding change. Fear is often one driving force. For me (as you'll see in my story), my change-averse nature was driven by a feeling of both deep dedication and dependence on my first job and organization, despite the issues that made me physically and mentally sick.

Eventually, I was able to resolve the fact that my identity is separate from that company and it was in my best interest to move on to my version of greater freedom. **When embraced instead of feared, relativity experiences make way for greater freedom in our careers and our lives.**

◆ ◆ ◆

Navigating Relativity

The five promises of relativity are inspiring motivators for taking the leap and embarking on a new job experience. Sometimes, a transition is thrust upon us; for example, if the organization closes or your job is eliminated. This presents a forced opportunity to embrace relativity and move on. However, it's not always so easy to know when to make a transition. A proactive transition to a new job can look like and feel like an escape. At some point, you might ask yourself: *When is the right time to move on when I feel the need to change?*

My first piece of advice is to identify and understand the core reason for why you are considering a transition. Embark on your relativity experience with intention. Maybe you need to move on in order to move forward and find more alignment with your current interests, fresh possibility, or greater potential. In that case, moving on is not an escape but a step forward.

Only you know why you're considering a transition. It takes a lot of introspection to get to the core driving motivator and your true intention for moving on. If you find that you're shying away from challenge, maybe it's right to stay and fight it out. If you're deprived of possibility, potential, and inspiration, it's likely time to move on.

After identifying your core intention behind your transition, the next challenge is to decide: When is the right time to move on? When change is not thrust upon us, we have to make the call as to when is the right time to move on. This is a call to take the lead and develop your own vision for your career path. Zoom out and envision your new normal. Design your boundaries and timeline for making the decision. Tell someone - a family member or friend - who can hold you accountable for identifying your intention and timeline.

Most people have one of two tendencies when it comes to transitioning jobs. One tendency is to procrastinate. Even though they know that they need a change and wake up each day thinking about it, they put it off for unknown reasons. This is why connecting to your core intention for wanting to move on, as well as your reasons for holding back, is key. Practicing patience and holding back on transitioning, even when you feel resistance to your current job, is not a bad thing. However, it's important to reflect and identify the real drivers of your unhappiness and develop a plan for finding a resolution. Listen to the signs and don't ignore the call to move forward.

Other people have the tendency to move on with too much haste. It's never a good idea to reactively move on when you feel resistance or anger toward your job (unless there is an emergency circumstance). Sometimes you can work to resolve the misalignment and find happiness in your situation again.

Before seriously considering a move, return to your interests, possibility, and potential. Get clear with yourself about the drivers of your unhappiness. With this clarity, you can then decide whether the root cause of the problem is solvable in your current job or not. Know that change is on the horizon and it's just a matter of time before you reach a resolution.

If you decide that it is time for a transition, begin your search starting with your interests (return to chapter 1). Interviews at other organizations are another great way to experience relativity because you learn what else is out there and go in with a clear intention to resolve your current issue by moving on. Enter each interview process with interests, possibility, and potential in mind. Make sure to choose a new position that aligns with your interests, fulfills your possibility needs, and fuels your potential. **It's better to take time off from work or find a part-time job than to hastily move on to a new full-time (a bigger committment) job that you don't love.**

Finally, the time between your current job and your next experience might be a good time evaluate if you are ready to embark on something all your own. This is what you'll learn to evaluate and practice in the next chapter, Synthesis. In my relativity story, I'll show how multiple apprenticeship experiences provided the fuel and inspiration I needed to move toward deeper self-awareness, purpose, and confidence to start something all my own.

◆ ◆ ◆

My Relativity Story

When I moved from Philadelphia to California to become a leader of a small team in a large retail company, I found that there was a great sense of possibility and potential for me. I felt supported by my leader and the company itself. My new leader listened to my suggestions and concerns. He took my feedback about everything from hiring, to processes, and scheduling. I found a renewed sense of hope in my abilities and my future.

Though there were many positive aspects of this new company and new environment, of course there were challenges as well. California was completely new to me and so different from the east coast. It took me about three months to really feel as though I had adapted to this new environment and culture. Similarly, learning an entirely new company culture and the inner-workings takes a lot of energy and effort. I enjoyed the learning process but had to practice patience and perseverance during this process of onboarding and taking responsibility for a whole new work scope and three team members.

After a few months, I realized that many of same leadership issues existed at this company that had existed at the company I had just left. My leader was very strong, experienced, and compassionate. However, many other leaders actually struggled to provide a vision for their team and break the vision down into clear individual responsibilities. Some of my peers, who were team members of these unorganized leaders, weren't sure what they were responsible for and complained about constant changes in priorities. It was difficult to work with teams that weren't aligned and organized about responsibilities and priorities. It made my team's work much more challenging and it held us back.

Another problem was that many leaders didn't provide enough acknowledgement or growth opportunities for their teams. Team members complained about the stagnant nature of the company and some people even left for other opportunities where they could learn more and grow. I was determined to not allow this stagnant or negative behavior to affect me or my team members. I would lead by example by remaining extremely clear, organized, and positive.

As a rookie leader, I could now empathize with the leaders who lacked techniques and guidance for how to lead. This was an important and pivotal awakening for me to realize that leadership was such a challenging transition for many people. I realized that I had found a trend: that even super-intelligent leaders often lack ways to align and engage their team members. Companies - even companies on opposite coasts with very different conditions and backgrounds - have similar challenges with leadership. **This common thread of leadership pain points opened my eyes to new problems and prompted me to develop my own solutions.** I couldn't escape the leadership problem just by moving companies; this common problem followed me and prompted me to come up with solutions.

Though there were leaders that didn't seem to know quite how to take the lead and succeed, there were also great leaders to observe and learn from at this company. Many leaders at the company were very successful in remaining productive and retaining their best team members. I saw how some leaders (like my own leader) spent time with their team members, communicated transparently, and provided opportunities for growth. These leaders had thriving teams that stayed dedicated and loyal to the company even through tough times. I saw how these leaders held the organization together in many ways and made consistent progress.

This was one way I learned how to lead and how not to lead. However, there were still some wide-open gaps in my knowledge; namely how to motivate my team and myself, how to develop my team members, and how to remain remain positive even through struggle. Aside from the leadership skills, internally I also faced some mental blocks to leading. **It seemed as though there were apparent contradictions between individual success and truly serving as a leader of others.** I was still looking for answers to my leadership puzzle.

After six months of working in this new job, I decided it was time for a much-needed vacation! I am not usually one to take many exotic vacations but I do love visiting family and friends. As a yoga teacher, I also love immersing in yoga trainings to continue my yoga education. So, I decided that it was time to visit India, the birthplace of yoga. I had never been to India (or Asia) before but I was ready for an adventure. I wanted to experience a new culture and environment because I was seeking some fresh inspiration and connection. I thought: *How awesome would it be to practice yoga in India with one of my favorite teachers?*

India sounded like a great idea, however, when it came time to actually book the trip and take the leap, I held back. Even though I would be traveling and practicing with one of my favorite yoga teachers in one of the most beautiful and safe places in India, I still hesitated to book. I feared facing so many unknowns in terms of travel, safety, and comfort. I had never been to Asia and I couldn't imagine what it would be like. *Would I be able to handle the environment? What if I got to the airport and they wouldn't let me in? What if I got bitten by something and couldn't find a legitimate hospital?*

I had never taken a vacation from work for more than three

days during my career so far. I didn't know if my job would even be there when I got back. *How would the work get done? Would my team remember me?* I was used to my routines and stability I had established. I loved my new life in California and I really didn't want to leave. But my intuition was telling me to do it! **I needed a break to rejuvenate and to resolve some of the leadership obstacles I was facing as a new leader.**

Finally, the day of departure came and I embarked on my first trip to India! It was the longest distance I had ever traveled alone. I traveled for 30 hours each way from my apartment, just north of San Francisco, all the way to the west coast of India. After taking a flight from San Francisco to Los Angeles, another flight from Los Angeles to the Middle East, and finally a flight to India, I took a 2-hour taxi transfer to the coast and arrived at the retreat center.

The next morning, I woke up to the sound of ocean waves crashing on the beach, a warm sea breeze, and the smell of the jungle. I met the rest of the group and we began a week of yoga and cultural immersion. The group was small, just about 12 people, but I found that the group was similar to the yoga community I had in Philly and in California. It was a tribe with the right vibe.

I definitely felt off center for the first few days. Between the jet lag and the new environment, I didn't quite feel like myself. It was the same discomfort I had felt when I started a new job and when I moved to California. It was the feeling of being out of my comfort zone.

The difference in climate was a challenge. It was hot and humid. I craved the cool breezes and dry heat of California. My yoga practice and the healthy vegetarian food at the retreat center helped me to acclimate and feel more energetic despite the heat. Eventually, I learned to adapt to the new conditions.

In yoga training, my teacher spent time teaching us yoga asana (poses) as well as philosophy. We talked about ethics, finding balance, and finding concentration through yoga and meditation. We focused on the importance of doing the self-work in order to lead by example in the world and embody what you believe in. These concepts and practices resonated as I thought about the questions and problems I faced as a leader. In this environment in India, my awareness of the teachings was sharper and I found new depth in my ability to reflect.

Soon, I started to relate what I was learning in yoga training to my leadership challenges at work. I realized that so many leaders in business needed to receive these teachings about ethics, self-reflection, clarity, and mindfulness. The yogic system of ethics, called the Yamas and Niyamas, gave me a proven system for resolving so many of the contradictions between my actions at work and my true intentions. These teachings helped me to get out of auto-pilot mode and wake up to what is most important.

This relativity experience helped me to realize that the real point of leading, for me, is to cultivate peace, progress, and genuine connections that benefit both the individuals and the collective. I felt like others needed to learn these teachings as well in order to find better alignment in their work and life.

While exploring and interacting with the people in India, I learned new ways of approaching life in a simpler and more mindful way that seemed to have deeper, more satisfying impact at the same time. I loved how the culture celebrated life for the sake of celebrating life, not necessarily for profit, results, or for recognition. I was working hard in yoga trainings - learning, practicing, and assisting. However, I felt more present and process-oriented, rather than completely results-oriented. I thought: *Wouldn't it be great if life at home and at work could feel like this, too?*

Though some of the western approach was there, I could see that the roots of so many of the practices and rituals I learned were rooted in deeper self-awareness, personal growth, and connection with others. **I found that I could use the philosophy I was learning and the culture as inspiration for shaping my leadership approach.** My team, as well as many other people, needed practices for bonding and celebrating wins just for the sake of celebrating and connecting. The culture and practices I fully immersed in while in India transformed my perspective of life and my approach to work.

My learnings from this trip to India filled the life and leadership gaps that western academia and corporate culture had no solutions for. The simple practices I learned for better focus, health, and joy were invaluable tools to add to my tool belt and share with others.

I found that when we take relativity leaps - whether to a new job or on a grand journey - we challenge ourselves to develop greater self-awareness, expand our capabilities, and discover creative solutions. **If I had not let go and taken the leap to visit an unknown place across the world, I would have never found the most unexpected and the most impactful solutions to my personal and professional challenges.**

When I returned to California, I looked the same. I went back to my usual work routine. However, all of that experience and new energy transformed the way I approached my work, which positively transformed the process and the results of my leadership and my career.

Letting go is something we often fear. However, relativity brings new space for opportunity and growth. Reaching for something higher is essential for personal growth and leadership in work and in life.

Relativity

in Action

Relativity Exercises

The three relativity exercises are a progression of exercises for helping you embark on experiences of relativity and document your new perspective. In the first exercise, you will return to your interests to reconnect to your intention. Then, in the second exercise, you will confront your fears (and reasons) for waiting to experience relativity. Finally, the third exercise is for identifying and reflecting on new realizations and how your perspective has changed after experiences of relativity.

These exercises set the stage for launching into a new experience of relativity. If you already have experiences of relativity, the third exercise will help you to reflect on your evolution and unique realizations. Let's go!

Exercise 1: Expand on your Interests

Exercise 2: Procrastination or Patience?

Exercise 3: Lenses of New Perspective

Supplies:

- Pen or pencil
- Paper
- Journal
- Black, red, green, blue, and orange pens (or pencils)

Relativity

Exercise 1: Expand on your Interests

Intention: Return to your interests to reconnect to how you are leading with your interests in your current work experience, which interests have been neglected, and how your interests have changed over time.

After experiencing the day-to-day at your job, evaluating the possibility and learning from potential opportunities, it's time to return to your interests. Have your interests changed throughout your work experiences? How? Maybe you already have this documented in your original interests map, or maybe your interests have even changed since then, and you need to document how they have changed.

In this exercise, you'll take a closer look at your interests and if/how they have changed since your first interests map in chapter 1. Relativity is all about fresh perspective and seeing through new lenses. This is an important exercise to return to and expand upon to prepare for Synthesis and Creativity in the following two chapters.

To begin, return to your original interests map to recreate your interests map from chapter 1 exercise 1.

View the color version of this exercise at:

www.awakeleadershipsolutions.com/awake-apprentice-exercises

Password: Apprent!ce

in Action

Example Interests Map from Chapter 1, Exercise 1:

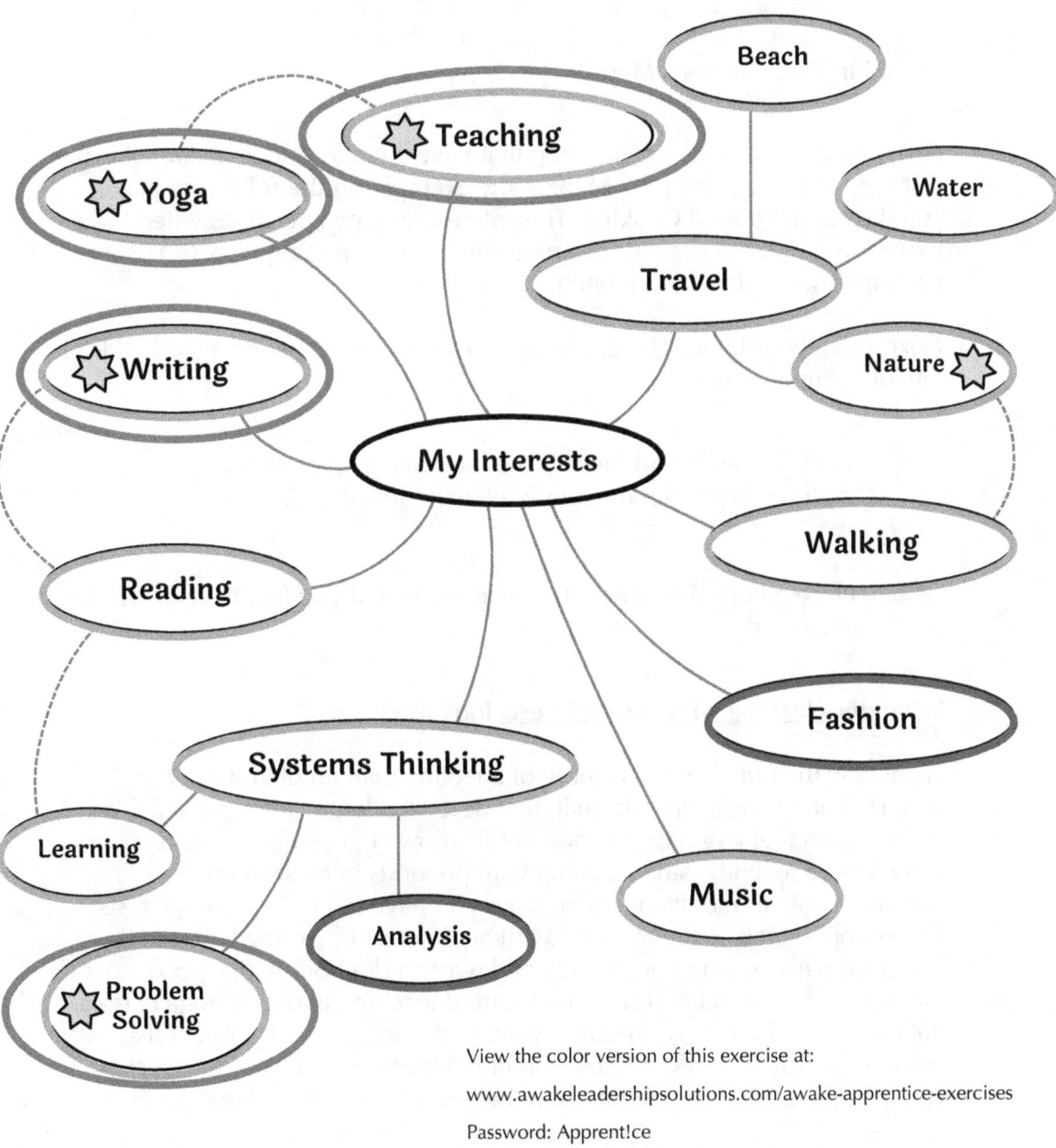

View the color version of this exercise at:

www.awakeleadershipsolutions.com/awake-apprentice-exercises

Password: Apprent!ce

Relativity

Exercise 1: Expand on your Interests

Updating Your Interests Map

First, add new interests to your map that have emerged since making the first version of your Interests Map. In my **example on the following page**, you'll see that I added Cooking. This interest emerged because, when I moved to California to work at a new company, one of my new rituals was cooking my own food more often.

Next, using your Interests Map, reflect on your work experience and add the following information:

 Place a check mark next to the interests that you feel you have really led with during your work experience.

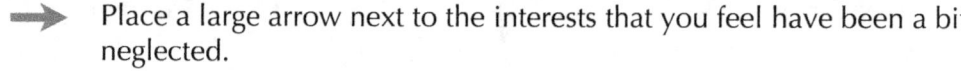 Place a large arrow next to the interests that you feel have been a bit neglected.

What does <u>leading with your interests</u> look like?

Leading with your interests is more of a feeling than an obvious act or gesture. The interests on your map that deserve a large check mark are the interests you feel you have become more knowledgeable about and experienced recently, since making your previous interests map. You should be able to identify tangible ways you have led with these interests. For example, I felt as though I led with my interest in writing because I practiced daily writing consistently and wrote a draft of my first book since making my previous interests map. I started teaching two new yoga classes, but I still think I could go further! Whether this experience happened at work or outside of work, it doesn't matter. However, you should feel that you are giving adequate attention to these interests. If not, give it an arrow.

in Action

View the color version of this exercise at:

www.awakeleadershipsolutions.com/awake-apprentice-exercises

Password: Apprent!ce

Relativity

Exercise 1: Expand on your Interests

Step 1: Use your previous Interests Map from chapter 1 or make a fresh Interests Map on the following page. Add new interests to your map that have emerged since making the first version of your Interests Map.

Use the space below to brainstorm what new interests have emerged and why.

_____

_____

_____

_____

Step 2: Next, using your Interests Map, reflect on your work experience and add the following information:

✓ Place a check mark next to the interests that you feel you have really led with during your work experience.

→ Place a large arrow next to the interests that you feel have been a bit neglected.

in Action

Your turn!

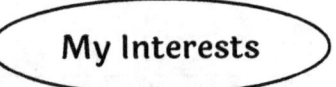

Relativity

Exercise 1: Expand on your Interests

1. Looking at your completed and marked-up Interests Map, answer: Which of your interests that spark your curiosity have you really led with in your work experience? How?

_____

_____

_____

_____

_____

2. Which of your interests that spark your curiosity have been a bit neglected? Why? What limitations in your current work opportunities or potential exist that keep you from leading with these interests?

_____

_____

_____

_____

_____

in Action

Exercise 1: Expand on your Interests

3. Looking at your completed and marked up map, what new interests did you add? As you can see, in my example, I added cooking.

_____

_____

_____

4. Considering your answer to question #2, how could you lead more with those important interests that have been a bit neglected? Is there anything you could do in your current job, at work or outside of work, to lead with these interests? How?

_____

_____

_____

_____

_____

_____

Relativity

Exercise 2: Overcoming Fear of Change

Intention: *Evaluate your current job and the current alignment with your interests, possibility, and potential. Move past fears and procrastination.*

This is a short but powerful exercise. When your work and home lives are busy, time often passes quickly and you'll lose track of your true intentions and level of contentment. Even when you know that change is needed, fear of change can be so strong that you'll procrastinate moving on or making a change.

In this exercise, you'll evaluate your current job's alignment with your interests, possibility, and potential. You'll confront any fears you might have about reaching further and gaining relativity experiences to move toward your creative potential. Answer the prompts. Expand in a journal.

How do you feel your current job aligns with your interests, fulfills your possibility needs, and helps you move toward your potential? How?

_____

_____

_____

_____

_____

_____

in Action

Exercise 2: Overcoming Fear of Change

If you were to rank the following three feelings how would you rank them from strongest to weakest? Rank your feelings of contentment, patience, and procrastination. Why is this your ranking?

_____

_____

_____

_____

If you chose procrastination as a strong feeling (rank 1 or 2), what are your fears around moving on or reaching for a new relativity experience? How could you stop procrastinating and lead with your interests, refill your possibility, and fuel your potential?

_____

_____

_____

_____

_____

Relativity

Exercise 3: Lenses of New Perspective

Intention: *Relativity is about gaining new perspective and evolving your approach to work and to life. Reflect on how experiences of relativity have changed your perspective on work and on life.*

When you transition to a second, third, or fourth (or more) job experience, it is important to document your new perspective and your learnings. A new work experience adds a new lens and we see universal challenges and situations in new ways.

New work experiences are experiences of relativity because we are exposed to new environments, new people, and different ways of doing things that prompt these "lens shifts" in perspective and help us to evolve.

In this exercise, I introduce four lens shifts that often happen as a result of relativity experiences. This profound exercise will help you to identify these lens shifts in your own experience, why they happened, and how they have changed your approach to work and life. This exercise will reveal your most profound, unique experiences and prepare you for Synthesis and Creativity.

Answer the prompts at the bottom of each page in a separate journal.

View the color version of this exercise at:
www.awakeleadershipsolutions.com/awake-apprentice-exercises
Password: Apprent!ce

in Action

Exercise 3: Lenses of New Perspective

Lens Shift 1: A More Vibrant and True Perspective

After one job experience, people often have a certain perspective of themselves and their work. However, after experiencing a second job, they have a whole new realm of experience and perspective because of this new imprint. **After two or more work experiences, the result is often a combination of two perspectives or "lenses".**

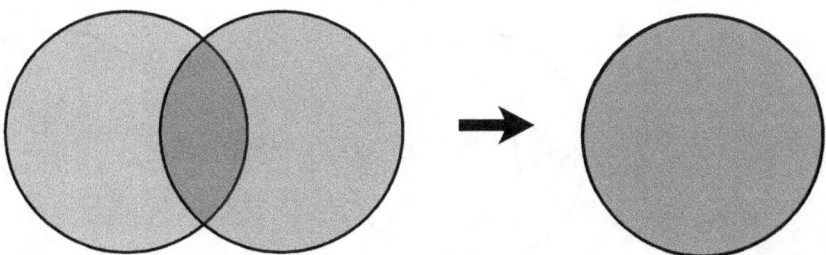

For me, an experience that shifted my perspective in this way was my first trip to India. Early in my career, I believed that work was meant to be only functional - that work was meant to even be painful and dreaded. However, visiting India taught me that even the most mundane tasks and activities can be made fun and engaging. I learned this from experiencing the culture. I still believed that work needed to be functional and effective. However, could it be functional and fun? With a bit of creativity and positivity, yes! I brought this newly formed perspective, which transformed my attitude and approach, to my second job and it made my work and my leadership much stronger.

What is a new experience - from your work or life - that transformed your pervious perspective?

Relativity

Exercise 3: Lenses of New Perspective

Lens Shift 2: A Removing a Dark Lens

With only one perspective, you might see situations at work and your own potential in a certain way. However, after gaining a new perspective through an experience of relativity, you might discover that a limiting belief about the world, your work, or yourself wasn't true. **A profound new work or life experience has the power to remove a blinder or dark lens from our mind's sight.**

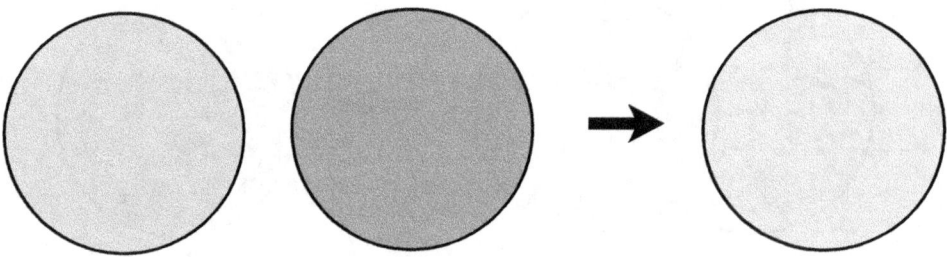

During school and my first job, I worked as though work was my identity. It was the central, primary thing that mattered in my life. When I found yoga and started practicing consistently, I learned that I had greater potential than merely my title, salary, and accomplishments at work. Work was important, but I had greater potential as a person to contribute to others in creative, deeply meaningful ways outside of my educational field and line of work. I started to explore and revisit the other parts of myself and other hidden potential, such as writing and teaching.

When has a brand new experience - work or life - removed a blinder or dark lens to make way for truth and potential?

Exercise 3: Lenses of New Perspective

Lens Shift 3: Replacing a Lens with a New One

The third way that relativity experiences can free a limited perspective is that they can totally change a current view of the world, our work, and ourselves. Have you ever experienced something that turns your perspective upside-down and changed you for good? **This is a shift that replaces our current perspective with a totally new perspective and approach, making our current perspective untrue forevermore.**

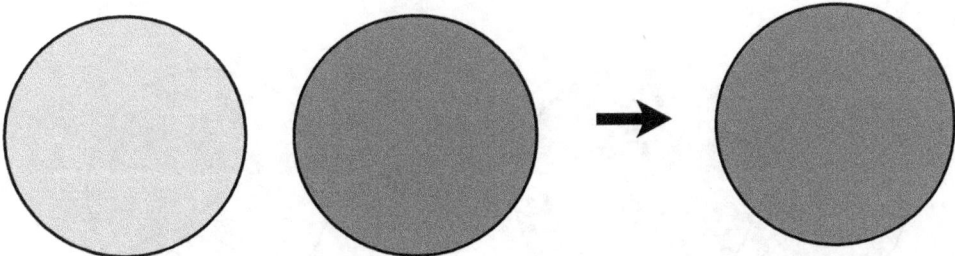

When I was told that I could work at a creative retail company, even as an engineer, and I experienced that first summer intenrship, my world was turned upside-down. I had previously thought that I had to work in computers, technology, or investment banking. While those seemed lucrative financially, they didn't interest me at all. When I found out that I could still work at a company with products that aligned with my interests, I gained new hope and a wider perspective for what is possible for me and my potential. I forevermore approached my career with an open mind for all possibilities - nothing is impossible!

When has a new experience - from you work or life - radically shifted your view and turned your perspective upside-down?

Relativity

Exercise 3: Lenses of New Perspective

Lens Shift 4: Perspective Remains the Same

Finally, sometimes a new perspective leaves us more confident in our current perspective. We should always be open to new experiences and how they might change us because relativity experiences can change us for the better. If we are not open to changing ourselves (or ourselves changing), we limit our potential. However, sometimes, **when we experience something new and even profound, we actually emerge with more confidence in our current perspective and approach.**

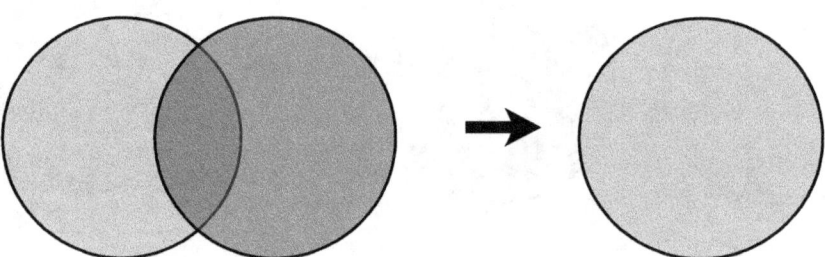

When I accepted a job at a brand new company in California and started work in a new environment, I was exposed to new approaches to leadership and new leadership challenges. Even though the leadership approach was a bit different from the approach I had experienced at my previous company, I still had the same perspective: that the same leadership challenges exist, despite different conditions. This new experience and perspective validated my already-formed belief that modern leaders needed more effective guidance and training that didn't yet exist.

When has a brand new experience - work or life - made you more confident in or validated your current perspective?

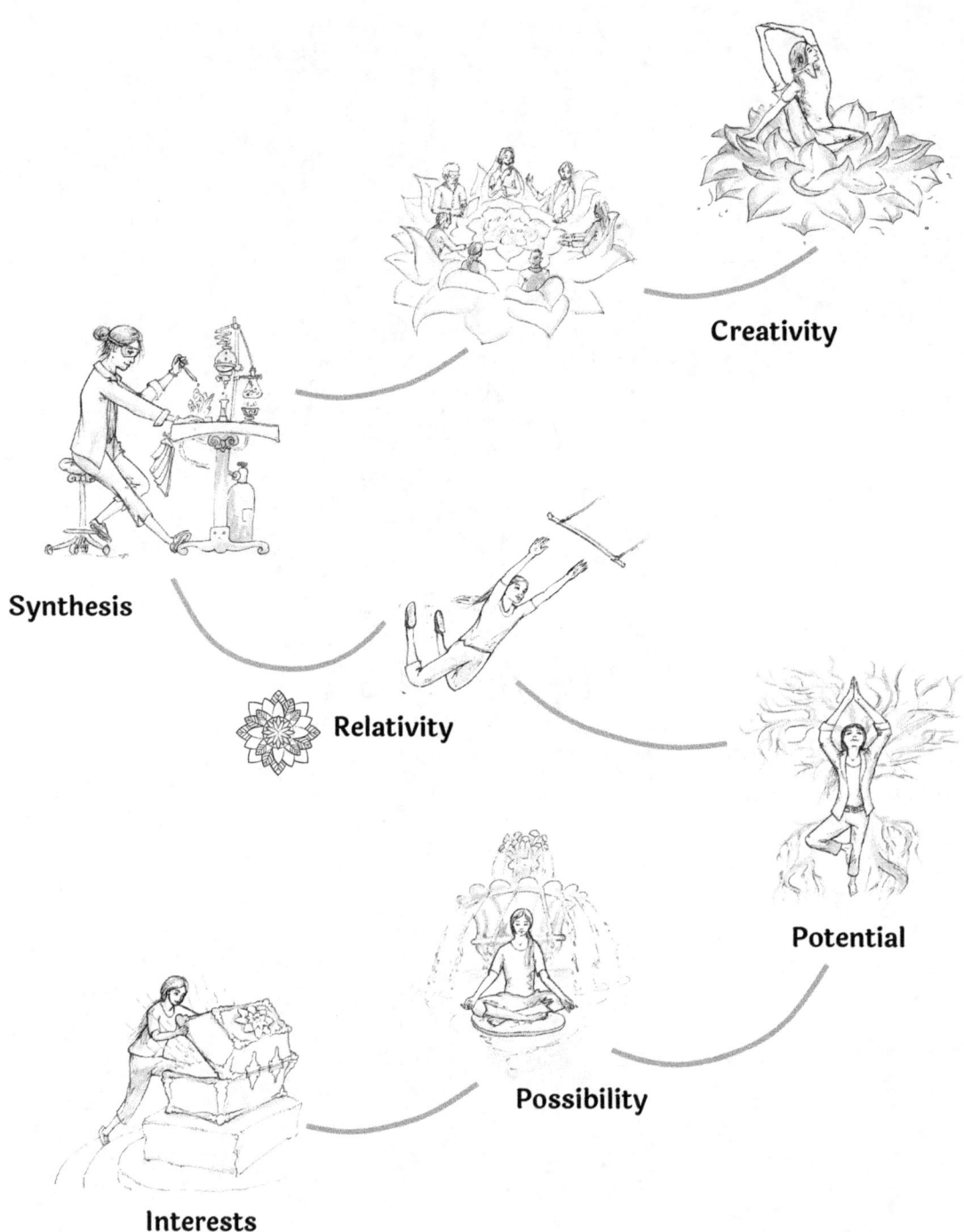

Earth to Creative Leader Tip #4

Make Graceful Transitions

Transitions between jobs are often overlooked due to excitement about the next opportunity. It's tempting to drop the ball and move on as quickly as possible once you've landed a new gig. This is totally normal; however, as I learned, graceful transitions are essential for real personal and professional growth. Transitions are the periods when you'll learn a lot about yourself and deepen your relationships with others (or not). When leaving a job, make sure to close loops and transition gracefully.

When transitioning, it's best to put yourself in the place of the next person. *What will they need to know? What is not documented that they will need to reference? What folders are messy?* Think about what you would like to know when entering a new job. Make sure the role is ready for the next person to take on smoothly. This is how an Awake Apprentice approaches a transition. Whether you return to the company or not, you will likely see some of your co-workers again in the future or need a reference from someone. Make sure to part with a reputation of professionalism and positivity. Finally, have coffee or lunch with your closest connections before you depart. Exchange contact information so you can stay in touch.

Up Next...

Are you ready to use your experiences of relativity and express your findings as new solutions and creations? In **Chapter 5, Synthesis**, you'll learn how to come up with new original ideas. Whether your ideas are solutions to add value at your current job or an idea for a venture all your own, synthesis is a powerful practice for moving toward creativity.

Chapter 5
Synthesis

Practice Synthesis

Synthesis is the act of combining or mixing different elements in order to form something new. For Awake Apprentices, synthesis is where interests, skills, and knowledge mix together to form new solutions, ideas, and creations. **The process of synthesis prompts you to use all the tools and relativity experiences that you have gathered along your Awake Apprentice journey.** In this chapter, you'll learn how to synthesize in order to come up with new ideas for original solutions and creations.

What is the difference between a solution and a creation? Solutions are the children of suffering, resistance, or obstacles. Along your journey as an Awake Apprentice, you'll likely learn about existing solutions as well as unsolved problems. On the other hand, creations are the children of voids, epiphanies, or opportunities. You'll also come across new ideas to expand on or build upon current products, processes, and services. The best solutions and creations are both functional and inspiring.

The ability to synthesize your career learnings and experience presents an opportunity to dig further into your independent potential and discover your purpose. Your ideas will be uniquely yours because your strengths and experiences are uniquely yours. Synthesis will be successful if you reflect on your unique path, challenges, and capabilities. No one's path is quite the same and therefore your approach to developing solutions and creations will be your own original contribution.

Sometimes synthesis happens naturally, all of a sudden. However, synthesis is not a passive or easy practice. Most of the time, synthesis involves spending time in deeper thought about your relativity experiences. While the path so far has been about gathering many different experiences of applied learning, synthesis requires space away from the activity to allow the experiences to combine and form into new ideas and solutions. To practice synthesis, an apprentice goes into his or her personal lab to reflect, experiment, and test new ideas.

Let's first look at how to develop a Synthesizer Mindset.

Synthesis is where interests, skills, and knowledge mix together to form new solutions, ideas, and creations.

How to Develop a Synthesizer Mindset

To cultivate the conditions for synthesis, an apprentice must approach each day and each situation with a Synthesizer Mindset. Some people naturally approach life with a Synthesizer Mindset because they were taught and encouraged to approach life with an open mind from a young age. **Synthesizers make connections between seemingly unrelated experiences.** They suggest opportunities and solutions rather than point out issues and problems.

Even if you don't feel like you are a synthesizer right now, there is still good news: We all have the ability to develop a Synthesizer Mindset. If you find yourself challenged when trying to problem solve or come up with original ideas, cultivating the qualities of a synthesizer is the first step in moving forward. Let's take a look at the three qualities of a Synthesizer Mindset and how to cultivate these qualities.

1: Live Life with an Open Mind

Every successful synthesizer operates with an open mind. This is easier said than done. Most people tend to default to their old ways of doing things, they believe there is one right way to do things, or they rely on the hard facts they know to be true. However, if you rely too much on the facts or the way something has always been done, you will rule out new opportunities for improvement. **A synthesizer is always open to and looking for new ideas, perspectives, and experiences.**

At work, you can practice having an open mind by entertaining new ideas from your team members and peers. If a peer or team member suggests an idea or wants to talk about a change, make the time to discuss it with them. Take a walk or meet for coffee outside of the office or usual work environment to talk about the idea. At first, this might seem like an activity that is tangent to your regular work and might be a waste of time. It will seem that way *until* you come across a great idea that improves your work and adds new value.

Outside of work, you can exercise an open mind by reading. Articles and books that are related to your work experience or area of interest often inspire ideas and new ways of thinking about problems. It's easy to search for books on Google, Amazon, or (my favorite) in your local bookstore. Browsing for new books in a store, away from the online advertisements and stimuli, allows you to tune in and gain deeper inspiration. There is something inspiring about surrounding yourself with books. It calms the mind and evokes a sense of curiosity.

Solutions to new problems require new ways of thinking and doing. Synthesis requires diverging from the usual, ordinary path and auto-pilot ways of thinking and working. By approaching work with an open mind, you'll lead by example in building a work culture of innovation and progress.

2: Make Connections Instead of Holding Experiences in Silos

For most of people, the brain is programmed to work like an organized filing cabinet with folders and walls. Work-related tasks and challenges are filed away in one area, personal challenges and experiences are filed into another area, and experiences in-between are often lost or logged in the subconscious. This system works wonderfully for task-oriented activities but presents a big obstacle when trying to synthesize.

Exercising an open-minded approach is like turning your mind into a big, open funnel. To practice synthesis, you must also be able to make connections between seemingly unrelated concepts and experiences. This involves flexing a different muscle in your brain to make connections between different categories of experiences and learnings.

Synthesis requires breaking down barriers and making connections between pieces of information in order to form new ideas. You have to actively break down the barriers by reflecting on your experiences, talking through alternative solutions, and experimenting.

To start connecting experiences and ideas that you might normally hold in separate silos, I suggest practicing daily free writing. Daily free writing is a powerful practice for reflection and for making connections between seemingly disparate ideas. As you continue to write daily about your experiences, feelings, obstacles, and ideas, you'll be surprised at how you naturally talk yourself through challenges and come up with creative ideas.

Also, be on the lookout for answers and ideas even in the most mundane or unplanned experiences. Don't have resistance toward the in-between moments or the unexpected events that happen along the route to your planned destination. This requires presence. Look up from your phone or, even better, put it away to fully experience each situation and conversation you are so lucky to have. People often miss opportunities and glaze over solutions because they are not present. A lack of presence numbs your creative abilities, too.

At work and in life, be fully present as much as possible. Don't hold experiences or information in silos. Practice presence and reflect on the experiences and the events you encounter, both planned and unplanned.

3: Be Solution-Centric Rather than Problem-Centric

Solution centricity is an essential practice for every Awake Apprentice to adopt and practice at work and in life. Have you ever worked with or taken class with someone who always complains about problems or points out problems but never proposes a solution? It's exhausting. When leaders and team members only point out problems and issues, they quickly become a burden for the team.

A solution-centric synthesizer always proposes a solution along with a problem. If you spot a problem, it means that you know there is a better situation than what is currently happening. There is an opportunity or solution to present along with every problem. Even if it's not do-able at that moment, it's about identifying something to start working toward. This approach turns every problem into an opportunity to practice problem solving, proactive leadership, and intentional action.

To practice solution-centricity at work, instead of just identifying the problem when you encounter one, also point out the better-case situation or solution. This is the first step in practicing solution-centricity. Then, form a plan for how to get to the solution. Envision the solution and the path for how to get there based on the current situation. If you don't have a proposed solution right away, propose a next step to resolve the problem and reach out to the right person to take it from there. Your leader and peers will appreciate if you present solutions and opportunities instead of problems.

For an Awake Apprentice, each opportunity to practice solution-centricity is an opportunity to practice problem solving. Problem solving requires using your knowledge, skills, and past experiences to form new ideas and solutions. **Solution-centricity is a lot about problem solving because you have to pull from your tool belt and past experiences in order to apply them to new situations and form original solutions.** You even get to see how your synthesis skills work in action and gather feedback to improve your approach.

Solution-centricity is also essential for Awake Apprentices because it requires positivity, confidence, and optimism. When you put yourself out there and suggest a way forward, it's bold and sometimes scary. However, practicing solution-centricity moves the team forward and allows you to exercise independent thinking. Don't be afraid to experiment. Put thought into your suggestions and ideas but don't hold back for too long. **Use work as a platform for experimenting with your best problem solving skills and solution-centric approach to work.**

When you present solutions and opportunities to talk through with your leader or peers, this brings positive energy instead of negative, stagnant energy to your work environment. Lead by example by practicing solution-centricity when faced with a challenge or problem.

Now you know the three qualities of a Synthesizer Mindset, but the environment and conditions around you are just as important for the process of synthesis.

◆ ◆ ◆

Setting the Conditions for Synthesis to Happen

Developing a Synthesizer Mindset allows you to gather new ideas, make connections, and practice problem solving. The next important aspect of synthesis is to set the conditions. **Fostering new ideas requires practices for preparation, a specific environment, and time.** Let's take a closer look at the how to set the conditions for synthesis.

To practice synthesis, you need to prepare with specific practices. When you're tired or stressed, it's almost impossible to think creatively about challenges. It's easy to complain and identify problems, but solution-centric thinking happens when you have an abundance of energy. To practice synthesis, it's important to hit the reset button and feel fully rejuvenated. The most fundamental preparation for practicing synthesis, both at work and at home, is sleep. Everything is easier with sleep, including synthesis. Sleep makes work easier because we feel more energetic and less stressed. Sleep rejuvenates our entire body, including our brain of course, and prepares us for deeper creative thinking.

Aside from sleep, the other essential practice to prepare for synthesis is some form of solo exercise or movement. Getting physical energy moving through your body prepares you for sitting and thinking deeply afterwards. Physical practices that help to cultivate the conditions for synthesis are different for each person. However, activities like yoga, walking, running, and meditation are some of the best. One hour of yoga and 20 minutes of meditation is my ideal routine for synthesis preparation. I often have my best ideas and realizations after a yoga practice and meditation session.

Now let's talk about the environmental factors. **Synthesis most often requires an environment that is peaceful because memories and ideas have to surface from the crevices of your mind.** Find an environment where you can sit peacefully and reflect, meditate, or write. Find environments that are both calming and inspiring, with minimal distractions. For some people, a peaceful and inspirational environment is a coffee shop, where there is music and where you can people-watch without having to interact or work. For others, peace is walking alone in nature. For me, a water view in front of the ocean allows my mind to relax and feel more expansive. Take time to figure out what environment cultivates peace for you and allows you to reflect, relax, and experiment.

Once you've found your optimal environment for synthesis, it's important to set aside the time for practicing synthesis. Though synthesis often happens naturally while we're at work or while our mind is relaxed at home, it also helps to spend intentional time on ideating, brainstorming, and experimenting. There is no specific time period that you should spend each day or each week on synthesis. However, you'll find that the longer you sit, reflect, and ideate, the deeper you'll get. There is so much gold in your mind. To get ideas flowing, try free writing, jotting down notes, or mind mapping. These are my favorite synthesis exercises.

The Process of Synthesis

Now, a few words about what actually happens after you cultivate the conditions for synthesis and set aside the time. When you sit down to think creatively or problem solve, the first 10 or 20 minutes is about getting through the day-to-day surface-level mind junk in order to get to those deeper ideas. Free writing helps to work through the surface-level mind clutter in order to get to more meaningful, creative challenges and ideas.

Original and exciting ideas will surface with time, as you spend more time in your synthesis lab. Give yourself dedicated time and space to reflect each day or each week. Allow your mind to unwind from the task-oriented activity to think big. Reflect on your experiences and actively focus on challenges and new ideas. I suggest setting aside at least 2 hours per week for intentional synthesis practice.

As opposed to intentional time to practice synthesis, synthesis also requires passive time and space. Though the right conditions and intentional focused time will encourage synthesis to happen, new ideas often take time to fully form. **Forcing a groundbreaking idea in a specific amount of time will cause stress and burnout.**

Just like a boiling pot of soup, synthesis requires heat *and* space. The intentional Synthesizer Mindset is the heat. You are putting the heat on to approach your work with a solution-centric mindset and draw on all of your experience to solve problems and create new things. However, in order for soup to cook, you have to cover the pot and allow it to cook on its own. After adding the ingredients and turning on the right amount of heat, you don't have a whole lot of control. You have to just give the soup space and time alone to cook so that all the ingredients simmer together to form something new and amazing. Similarly, we need space and alone time in order to Synthesize.

Synthesis is an active practice that requires space and patience. Ideas that you set goals or forecasts around will be very unoriginal, clearly forced ideas. They will likely be obvious and not very creative. Keep showing up to brainstorm. Give your ideas space to grow and improve with time.

◆ ◆ ◆

Common Synthesis Blocks

Even with the best intentions for practicing synthesis, sometimes it's still challenging and it feels like rolling a boulder up a hill. Let's take a look at some common synthesis obstacles.

The first obstacle many Awake Apprentices encounter is that they don't know where to start. *What will I write about? What should I focus on when I brainstorm or ideate?* This is really up to you. Sometimes it's best to not have anything specific to focus on so that you can really listen and allow challenges and ideas to surface naturally when given the space and time.

If you need a place to start, try starting with a problem statement or a challenge you're facing in life or at work. For example, if a customer recently filed a specific complaint about a product or purchase, start with this as your problem statement and spend the ideating solutions. *How could you resolve the issue? How can you prevent this issue from happening going forward?* Write down the problem statement and your solutions. Use your solution-centricity and problem solving skills.

Another approach is to begin with a quote. Choose your favorite quote or a quote you came across recently. Use the quote to inspire your writing, problem solving, or a new idea or work of art all together. *Why does this quote resonate with you? How does the quote come to life in your everyday life?* Spend 30 minutes just writing a response to the quote.

A second common obstacle (maybe the most common for Awake Apprentices) is addiction to work mode. I also call this "operating on the yo-yo". I call it that because even when you try to take a break or distance from work mode, your mind returns to it. You crave the work-related activity of doing, doing, doing. You simply can't detach from the yo-yo to allow your mind to relax. *Have you ever felt this way? Do you have a friend that can't stop working, even when they don't really need to?*

Sometimes, Awake Apprentices love work so much that they do it all the time, even at home. However, usually the real reason is that their mind loves something to cling on to. When someone feels bored or lonely, work is an easy outlet to go to in order to always have something to do and to feel useful and purposeful. This isn't a bad thing, but it can become a bad thing if you become your work! It can even get to the point where your mind needs work to cling onto, and it becomes an addiction.

It's important to find a balance between work and life, and between task-oriented work for someone else and moving further toward your own independent potential. This is easier said than done in our hyper-connected world full of easy access to e-mail and news. **It's almost impossible to practice synthesis while engaged with requests or with a mind full of to-do's.** In intense execution mode, focused on a task and a result, the mind shuts off to new ideas and connections.

Put aside that intentional time for synthesis by preparing and finding the right environment. Put your phone on silent and put all of your technology out of sight and out of mind (or at least turn off the WiFi if you ideate with your computer). Once you get in the zone and start ideating, it's a lot of fun and very fulfilling. It takes dedication to practice synthesis, especially when it requires a change in your regular schedule or mindset in order to make the time. However, it's worth it! Your creations and solutions will only form and come to life if you practice synthesis. **Put aside the time and find space to practice synthesis and create the boundaries you need to ideate free from the constant connectivity.**

Finally, a third obstacle that gets in the way of practicing synthesis is fear. There are two types of fear that are most common for Awake Apprentices. The first is imposter syndrome, which stems from lack of confidence and fear of failure. Awake Apprentices that have been working for a strong leader or impressive, large company often question why they would be smart or creative enough to come up with a brand new solution or an idea. When you haven't fully seen or expressed your independent potential before, it's hard to envision what that looks like and believe that it's realistic.

To overcome this first type of fear, consider: *How do you think the people that invented the most prized innovations and most inspiring works began?* They came up with an idea and started experimenting. They put it out there and invested in their own potential. As an Awake Apprentice, you have plenty of interests and experiences to work with. **Don't get in your own way of practicing synthesis and unleashing your creative abilities. Believe in yourself and get started.**

The second type of fear stems from the perception that synthesis is stealing. *Isn't synthesis a form of stealing two or more ideas and making a new one?* No, synthesis is not stealing because the experiences are yours and the ideas are coming from your own experiences. Many of our most treasured products and services resulted as a form of synthesis of a problem that clearly existed and a solution from a seemingly unrelated realm or another product. Most creators do not come up with something that magically pops into their head, out of nowhere. Most creators develop something related to past experiences and inspiration.

To overcome this second type of fear, think of synthesis and creating as giving. We need solutions and new creations in order to evolve. Ultimately, it's about the intention you have. If you intend to steal in order to make money or gain recognition, then yes, you are probably just stealing and recycling other people's ideas and works. If it is truly original, born from synthesis, with the intention to provide something of value for others, it is yours to create and to give. Synthesis is all about giving. It's about giving yourself new and independent potential. It's about giving new potential to the world.

My Synthesis Story

When I returned to California after my first trip to India, I had even more gratitude for my daily writing. I had fresh energy to put behind my writing and so many ideas to write about. Each morning, I would wake up, do some light yoga, make my coffee, and sit down to write for 30 minutes. To really write and practice synthesis, I needed an environment and practices that sparked both focus and inspiration. I sat in my small, quiet kitchen facing the window. I used writing to dig into my psyche, problem solve, brainstorm new ideas, and give myself much-needed pep talks. I'd review my work progress from the previous day, reflect on my challenges, and mentally prepare for the day ahead.

When I'd tell family and friends about my morning routine, they'd ask me how I had time for it. My answer: I make time because it is worth it. I needed this time each morning for reflection and preparation. **Writing wasn't just a practice for my own mental sanity and productivity; I found that it was actually essential for my leadership.** I could better support my team when I took time to prepare, center, and express myself each morning before engaging with my team members. I'd show up to work with clarity about what my priorities were and how I would approach challenging situations.

Writing helped me find my voice as a leader. I learned, through experience and reflection, that I was often my own best advisor. The way to solve problems was not to always ask others for direction or validation, but instead to practice reflection and thoughtful discernment. I sometimes sought advice from respected peers, influencers, and leaders. However, as the one closest to my experience and closest to my team, I often knew the best solution given my perspective and experience. I found that free writing was an essential practice for synthesis. I became a stronger problem solver and a more creative thinker and doer.

One morning while free writing, I was problem solving my way through a teamwork situation. This situation had been brought to my attention by one of my best team members, Jason, during our one-on-one meeting the previous afternoon. Jason was frustrated because another team member, Mark, was taking credit for his work in group meetings and on group e-mail threads. Although I had a lot of other work to do, I knew that I needed to pay attention to this and resolve the issue because it was clearly a demotivating distraction for Jason, one of my best team members.

That same week, I had been studying an ethical concept from yoga philosophy called Non-Stealing. The principle of Non-Stealing says that, to practice ethical behavior toward ourselves and others, we must refrain from stealing material things, acknowledgement, and opportunities from others. When we steal, we take away someone's energy (no matter the form) that they need in order to do their best work. This is unethical because it harms on an individual level and a collective level, in terms of peace and progress.

I realized that the key word, or form of energy, Jason identified as lacking was *acknowledgement*. While the work was ultimately still getting done and the team was making collective progress, I could tell that Jason craved fair acknowledgement. With fair acknowledgement, he would be more focused and motivated. *Did Mark even know that he was acting unethically?* Maybe not. He didn't seem to actually want to cause harm to anyone else on the team.

To fix the issue, I decided to do two things. First, I designed a short activity for our team meeting. The activity was an exercise for positive acknowledgement. I gave out notecards and we each wrote down a positive acknowledgement for each other person on the team. The positive acknowledgement was for anything relevant - completing a project, providing help with a task, taking on extra work, engaging with a positive attitude, or running a meeting smoothly. This exercise helped get everyone into in the practice of giving positive praise to others to cultivate connection and motivation.

This was a good first step in solving the issue, but there was still work to do. Next, I used team meetings to regularly facilitate discussion about our recent progress and milestones as team.

We reviewed our wins and acknowledged each person for their contributions. As we reviewed the progress, I realized that Mark sometimes acknowledged others for their work and sometimes he did not. There were a few situations where I had to pause and say, "Mark, wait, *who* followed through and took that call?" Or, "Mark, *who* found the error and fixed it?" I was gently realigning reality for the team to get everyone on the same page and intentionally practice Non-Stealing. We still gave acknowledgement all around. Each team member was positively acknowledged for many things. However, each team member needed to acknowledge reality and ensure that everyone was on the same page about who contributed each component of the milestones.

While it might at first seem time consuming or trivial to do these exercises, I realized that fair positive acknowledgement is really important at the individual level. Without fair individual acknowledgment, the whole team suffers as people lose motivation and respect. I remembered, from my past and present, how unfair it felt when someone stole positive acknowledgement from me. I realized how positive reinforcement meant so much to me as a team member in providing motivation. I was so glad when my previously frustrated team member reported back that things had improved since our team meeting discussion and with the continuation of these team meeting exercises.

This was one of the first instances where I clearly remember applying yoga philosophy to my work experience. I was synthesizing! Yes, I could have *maybe* resolved this issue without it, but yoga philosophy provided simple and clear guidance for how to approach my leadership obstacle with a logical yet soulful solution.

My morning writing sessions continued to serve as a platform for breaking down barriers between information and for brainstorming to come up with solutions to my leadership challenges. It was a safe space for diving deep into my psyche for answers to unresolved situations and questions both at work and in my life. It was a place I could be open-minded and solution-centric. The best part was that work provided the opportunity to test out my solutions in practice and to iterate. This was an experience of applied learning, where I was able to practice synthesis and exercise my ability to problem solve.

A few months passed and some of my peers - fellow leaders - started asking me how I kept my team both aligned and motivated, even through challenging times. *How do I delegate clearly, despite constant change? How do I keep my team motivated, no matter the task or work scope?* These were big questions but we were clearly doing something right. I thought, there must be a way to describe how we were actually doing it in practice. I tried my best to write down everything I did and how I did it.

One weekend, I sat at a picnic table for almost two hours mind mapping and writing notes about all the leadership practices and yoga philosophy concepts that helped me to manage my team and my work. I almost filled my journal with practices and exercises. It was a mess but it was a start. I organized and reorganized the information. I realized that my methodology had started to take the form of a system of different leadership vitals and exercises. Some of the exercises were important for articulating the team vision. Some exercises were important for fueling inspiration. Some exercises were for optimizing our tools and making sure we had the right knowledge about how to use them. After countless planned and unplanned synthesis sessions, the system started to take form.

My writing practice served as a platform for practicing synthesis. **Practicing synthesis allowed me to integrate all of my experiences and knowledge in order to come up with solutions and ideas.** Now: *How would I actually turn this idea for a leadership and teamwork system into something functional for other people to learn from and use?* The next challenge was to tap into my creative powers in order to give form to this idea. That's exactly what I'll show you how to do in the next chapter, which is all about the creative process. Before you move on to the final chapter, make sure to work through the three synthesis exercises.

Synthesis

in Action

Synthesis Exercises

Awake Apprentices synthesize to come up with new ideas by focusing on functional and inspiring ideas, using a solution-centric mindset, and continuously generating ideas. The three synthesis exercises will help you generate new, powerful ideas. In the first exercise, you'll identify products, services, and experiences that you find functional and inspiring. The second exercise will prompt you to use your work experience to apply your solution-centric mindset. Finally, the third exercise will prompt you to generate new ideas of your own!

Exercise 1: Functional or Inspiring?

Exercise 2: Solution-Centric Mindset

Exercise 3: Put 20 Ideas to Paper

Supplies:

- Pen or pencil
- Paper
- Journal

Synthesis

Exercise 1: Functional or Inspiring?

Intention: Define functional versus inspiring for yourself using real-world examples. Hone in on what you believe is meaningful to work on and share with the world.

In this exercise, you will look outside - to existing products, services, and experiences - to define the difference between functional and inspiring. Ideas that are unique and creative often solve a problem and inspire the user. The best products, services, and experiences are both functional and inspiring.

If you think about it, you could really categorize any product, service, or experience as functional, inspiring, or both! It's all based upon your preferences, needs, and perception of value.

This exercise serves three purposes: to gain awareness of your perspective, to gain empathy for others (understanding that they might have other preferences), and to define what functional versus inspiring means to you. Ultimately, this exercise will provide the foundation for getting intentional about your ideas and the way in which you manifest your creative contributions. Let's begin!

in Action

Exercise 1: Functional or Inspiring?

Functional products, services, and experiences

Functional products, services, and experiences serve a function. They get you from point A to point B. You need them and use them for a reason (usually). However, you might not necessarily *enjoy* using them. They are not a source of daily happiness, connection, or inspiration. For me, examples of functional things are my refrigerator (product), my car (product), and visiting the DMV (service). I need to use these things, but I don't necessarily *enjoy* the experience.

What are products, services, and experiences that are **functional** for you? Write down at least three and why they are only functional for you.

Synthesis

Exercise 1: Functional or Inspiring?

Inspiring products, services, and experiences

Inspiring products, services, and experiences obviously, well, inspire you. They enhance your day-to-day lifestyle in some way, and keep your energy and mood uplifted. They aren't functional per-se; if you don't have it you won't die, but you do value them and need them. For me, inspirational things are fresh cut flowers, live concerts, and horoscopes. I don't necessarily *need* these things, but I really *enjoy* them.

What are products, services, and experiences that are **inspiring** to you? Write down at least three and why they are inspiring.

_____

_____

_____

_____

_____

_____

_____

in Action

Exercise 1: Functional or Inspiring?

Functional, Inspiring, or Both?

Products, services, and experiences that are functional and inspiring are things that are a necessity for you and you enjoy. Remember that this is based on your perspective - someone might find a leaf blower really inspiring and someone might absolutely need fresh-cut flowers to do what they do each day. For me, things that are both functional and inspiring are yoga, books, and the Golden Gate bridge. I need these three things to feel good day-to-day, to learn, and to do my best work. I also enjoy using and/or doing them! They cultivate deeper connection, happiness, and inspiration for me.

What are three products, services, or experiences that are **functional and inspiring** to you? Why?

_____

_____

_____

_____

_____

_____

_____

Synthesis

in Action

Exercise 2: Solution-Centric Mindset

Intention: *Hone in on your current work experience and identify solutions to common or reoccuring problems to develop a solution-centric mindset.*

Every day, you probably encounter challenges, obstacles, issues, and problems at work. You encounter them yourself, you encounter them with your team, you observe organizational issues, and you hear about obstacles that peers and friends face. Some problems are easy to solve. Other problems are ongoing issues that persist. Awake Apprentices are successful because they use these problems as prompts or opportunities to practice **problem solving**.

In this exercise, you will identify problems you face, organizational problems, or problems friends and peers are facing. Then, with the visual guidance of the exercise, you'll formulate your own solutions.

Turn the page to begin!

Synthesis

Exercise 2: Solution-Centric Mindset

Problem ➡ Solution

Every problem deserves a solution. Some problem-solving opportunities play to our interests, strengths, and capabilities more than others. Use the following pages to document at least two current challenges you are facing at work, or challenges you observe at work. Then, on the opposing matching side, propose a solution.

Make sure to clearly and concisely define the problem. This can be an exercise in itself. Then, propose one or more solutions and choose which one you'd ultimately suggest. In the Notes area, identify which solution you think is best and within your control to execute.

Example:

Problem	*Solution(s)*
Engineering teams are not communicating effectively, and they are not meeting objectives on time or to specificaitons.	1. Daily morning meeting with cross-functional teams to review progress and day's plan 2. New engineering manager 3. Team events to form better bonds and connection 4. Incentives for meeting objectives

in Action

Exercise 2: Solution-Centric Mindset

Problem ➡ Solution

Your turn!

Problem	*Solution(s)*

Notes:

_____

_____

_____

Synthesis

Exercise 2: Solution-Centric Mindset

Problem ➡ **Solution**

Your turn!

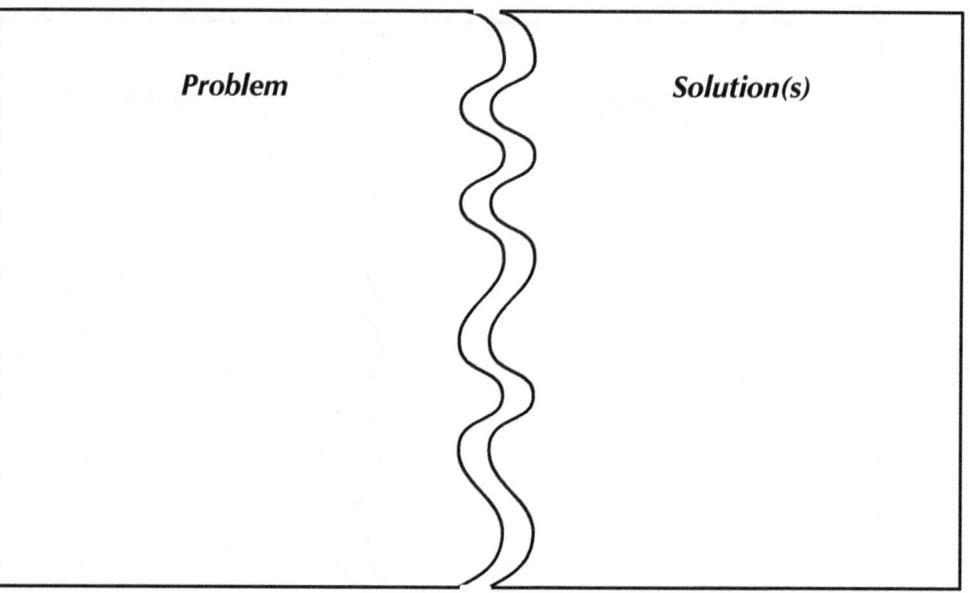

Notes:

_____

_____

_____

in Action

Exercise 3: Put 20 Ideas to Paper

Intention: Come up with 20 ideas in order to get your ideating muscles working and tap into your creativity. Build on your relativity experiences and insights.

In this exercise, you will come up with 20 original ideas based on your work and life experience and observations. You have all you need. Your apprenticeship(s) and observations in the preceding four chapters have prepared you for this important exercise.

At first, it can be challenging or even scary to come up with your own ideas. People often make excuses for putting this kind of opportunity aside and they go back to their more predictable work. However, this kind of work is the most important.

In your first round of 20, your ideas might seem shallow or too similar to things that already exist. That's totally normal. You are burning off surface-level thoughts and influences. Once you begin to write down your own original ideas every week, your ideas will get better and better. They will become more original and you will realize the power you have to come up with original solutions to the problems you face and develop new creative ideas.

I only provide space in this book for your first week of 20 ideas. I suggest also using a separate journal to document your 20 ideas each week going forward. Set a weekly reminder to spend 30 minutes on generating new ideas to exercise your synthesis muscle.

Turn the page to begin!

Synthesis

Exercise 3: Put 20 Ideas to Paper

Your turn!

Begin listing your ideas below. Refer to your Interests Map, as well as exercises 1 and 2 for inspiration.

in Action

Exercise 3: Put 20 Ideas to Paper

Continue to ideate here or in a separate journal.

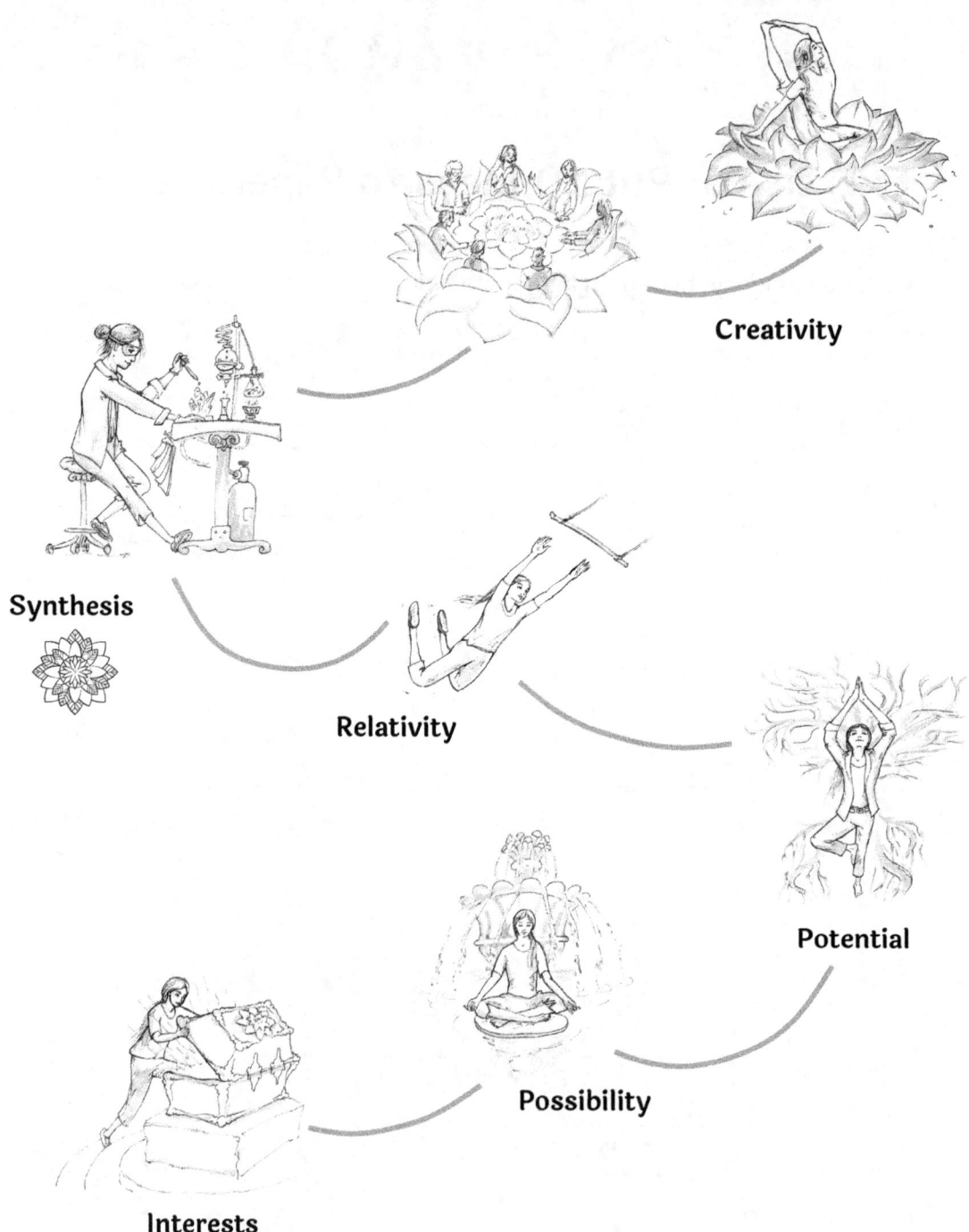

Earth to Creative Leader Tip #5

Stay Social

When practicing synthesis, it's easy to get stuck in the lab and never emerge. It's exciting to work on new ideas, so spending time alone becomes the norm. However, it's important to stay social and make like-minded connections.

Spending time with other people is essential for mental health. Sometimes it feels as though people drain your energy or take away your creative spirit. These are the wrong kinds of people to hang out with. **Find people that encourage your creativity and give you energy.** This energy will enhance your ability to synthesize.

Secondly, like-minded friends and collaborators are great for idea sharing and feedback. It's fun to brainstorm with people to come up with new ideas, especially when you find yourself in a creative rut. Staying in touch with "thinking" people and staying social at least weekly helps to keep in touch with reality. If you hide away too long, you'll start you lose touch with reality and your creations will not be applicable or as powerful.

When you share ideas with like-minded people and observe how others perceive your ideas, your ideas often grow and evolve faster. The breaks to spend time with others serve as time to refresh and rejuvenate. You'll return to your solo practice of synthesis with fresh ideas and energy.

Up Next...

In the **sixth and final chapter, Creativity,** you'll learn how to put your ideas into action! Execution and follow-through are challenging but essential for putting your creative contributions out into the world. Turn the page to begin awakening your creative potential.

Chapter 6
Creativity

Awaken Your Creativity

When you think of someone who is truly Creative, who comes to mind? It's subjective, as are most things in life, but note *who* comes to mind first for you and *why* they are creative in your opinion.

We often think of creative people as the dreamers and disrupters of society. Creative people have vibrant imaginations. As an Awake Apprentice, you have started using your imagination by practicing synthesis. Synthesis allows you to imagine what is possible and how you can use your learnings and experience to solve problems and add value.

Creative people are disruptive because the ideas they contribute are original. Disruptive ideas challenge the status quo and replace outdated products and processes with new, fresh solutions. Not all disruptive ideas are successful because creativity involves risk and experimentation; however, disruptive ideas are often what we need most in order to move forward as a society.

Creative people are also doers! This is key for our work in this chapter. **Successful creative people don't just talk about their ideas, they actually bring them to life.** It's challenging to follow through on execution and iteration, but this process transforms an idea into an impactful contribution.

Creativity is the destination for Awake Apprentices because it is where your ideas become real solutions and contributions. The creative process is the vehicle for turning your big ideas into actual offerings. Through the creative process, Awake Apprentices develop products, services, and experiences that evoke happiness, inspiration, and connection.

Creativity is the destination for Awake Apprentices because it is where your ideas become real solutions and contributions.

What really qualifies as Creative?

There are often disagreements about what is truly creative or what creativity really means. As I mentioned, creativity is subjective. However, there is also a lot of misunderstanding about what is truly creative. Someone might successfully *create* something but that does not mean it is *creative*. For our purposes, a creative contribution has three basic attributes:

Original: The idea has never been manifested before in this specific form, with this specific impact.

Functional: It serves a core purpose for someone. It solves a problem or adds value.

Inspiring: It evokes happiness, joy, and connection.

As you already know from the synthesis chapter and exercises, some products and services serve a basic, functional need. Though functional products and services are needed, they often seem like necessary evils that actually reduce happiness, inspiration, and connection in the short-term or the long-term.

Truly creative people develop products, services, and experiences that offer a functional benefit but also spark inspiration, joy, connection, and happiness. When creating something new, you can think of this marriage of functionality and inspiration as **Functional Art**. This term has helped me as a creative entrepreneur to shape my offerings in ways that serve a need and spark inspiration. It is a reminder that though we have basic physical and mental needs, the spiritual aspect is always important as well. Keep this concept of Functional Art in mind as you design and execute your own creative works.

Does everyone actually have the ability to be Creative?

For some people, creativity is an inherent strength. However, for most of us, we have to intentionally strengthen our creative abilities. The Awake Apprentice journey is the preparation you need for manifesting your own creative works because you have the practical knowledge and experience from the field that will provide inspiration for new solutions and offerings.

I use the word *"manifest"* in this section as opposed to *"build"* when speaking about creative works because a creation can really be anything - a painting, a software solution, a vehicle for transportation, a book, an appliance, a culinary creation, a festival, a class, and more. Many people often doubt their creative abilities because they believe they don't have the skill of a painter or the mind of a poet. Even with the mind of an engineer or an accountant, you can still manifest creative works. These industries are actually some of the industries that could benefit from creativity the most!

Some of us learn to be creative as kids but then we are not encouraged to be creative as adults. We're told to take a safe route by doing something very logical and embarking on a linear career path. I call this the **Conveyor Belt**. The conveyor belt seems safe because it takes us down a previously charted path at a safe speed. However, the conveyor belt does not lead toward a more interesting or necessarily impactful career. Instead, staying on the conveyor belt can actually numb our creative abilities if we don't intentionally use our work experience as an experience of applied learning.

Creativity is the practice for coming up with a vision (or form for the idea), designing the plan, and executing the work. Creativity requires both vision and execution. **I believe that creativity can be cultivated and strengthened through the practices and steps detailed so far in this guidebook.** So, yes, I believe that everyone has the ability to be creative in his or her own authentic way. Let's now take a look at how to actually manifest your creative ideas.

The Process: Manifesting Your Creative Ideas

To *manifest* an idea is to turn a theoretical idea into a tangible form. To manifest your idea, you must take your idea and turn it into a product, service, or experience that people can use and enjoy.

The best ideas and creations often emerge naturally from challenging experiences and intrinsic motivation. However, there is also intentional work involved in manifesting creative solutions. Let's take a closer look at how to practice your creativity and bring your ideas to life.

1. Return to Your Skills and Strengths

When deciding how to manifest your idea, start by reflecting on your core skills and strengths. **It's important to consider the skills and strengths you use at work, as well as the skills and strengths you use in your personal life.** Think through a typical day or week and write down the skills and strengths you used. Reflect back on your career so far and write down which skills and strengths you have built over time.

It's often hard to identify your unique skills and strengths after working in an organization for a long period of time. Working in a large corporation or even on a small team often results in a very specific skill set and narrow view of what we're capable of accomplishing. You might see yourself as part of a greater whole, dependent on others. It's true that you're always part of a greater whole, whether it's a team, a company, or society; however, it's important to acknowledge your own independent skills and strengths because this builds confidence and gives you the foundation for putting your ideas into action. You're more powerful than you might give yourself credit for.

While reflecting on your skills and strengths, you might also feel that you don't have a skill set that is creative. When I wanted to manifest my own creative project, I felt as though I had no skills at all that would allow me to make something creative. I could organize and optimize a spreadsheet model, I could plan, and I could cook... But, I didn't know how to draw. I didn't know how to sew. I had no design skills. I didn't know how to film. At the time, I felt like I didn't *really* know how to write. I was stuck. However, as you'll see in my story, when I approached my creative work with more optimism and compassion toward myself, I was able to discover my depth of creative skills.

There are so many ways of manifesting original ideas as products, services, and original works that we often can't imagine until we think differently, outside of the box. I realized that my personal writing practice was indeed writing, even if I wasn't a professional writer (yet!). Writing was (and is) one of my core creative skills. I realized that I practiced design when I crafted gifts for people, cooked new dishes, and decorated my apartment. I was (and I am) a skilled designer, even if I could benefit from some more practice. I was solution-centric in that I'd help others at work and in life to come up with solutions to move forward. I had more creative skills and strengths than I gave myself credit for initially.

Even if you think that your skills, strengths, and experiences don't relate to producing something creatively on your own, start from where you are. Think about all the capabilities you've developed throughout your apprenticeship experiences. Acknowledge the skills and strengths related to your work experience. **Also think about the skills and strengths you've developed through life experience.**

2. Identify the Form

After identifying your current strengths and skills, it's time to hone in on the vision for how you will manifest your idea. Will your creation be in the form of a piece of clothing, a board game, a website, a book, a song, or something else? The form that your idea takes is important for checking the boxes of both functionality and inspiration. The format should fulfill the utility you hope to achieve and it should add beauty to the world. Products, services, and experiences that achieve a goal in terms of functionality but don't inspire actually deter people from using them. Differentiate by adding an authentic, creative cool factor to your format.

You can see examples of how companies like Patagonia, Tesla, Anthropologie, and Apple make products that both serve a functional purpose and have unique, inspiring design that makes the experience enjoyable. Small companies do this, too. In my town of Marin, a coffee shop called Equator achieves the functionality and inspiration balance by offering excellent coffee while having a cool, uniquely branded concept from their cups to their store interior. **It requires deep reflection and experimentation to find the right form for your creation but the form is part of what makes your product or service spark happiness, connection, and inspiration.**

There are many ways to manifest your creations as products, services, or experiences. The process of figuring out the right form for your idea is a process of looking outward, then inward, then outward, then inward again. Let me walk you through what I mean.

Look outward. *How are others in your field of interests or others with an idea like yours manifesting their idea?* It helps to first look outward for two reasons. One reason is that others who are already on the path but a little ahead of you as far as manifesting have figured out a way to do it. Observing how others manifest their creations gives you an idea for what can be done. The second reason is because it allows you to differentiate and make your creation more authentic and uniquely yours. I call this practice Comparative Analysis. You have an advantage, in a way, because you can use their example as a means for deciding what aspects you would change to fit your idea and authentic concept. Do your field research by observing products and services in the same field. See how they manifest their ideas as solutions and new offerings.

Look inward. *How can you use your skills, strengths, interests, and experiences to bring your idea to life? How will your unique Awake Apprentice journey be reflected in the form?* Looking inward means spending time alone to brainstorm the format on your own. When brainstorming about the form, first return to your interests. Choose what would feel authentic as a vehicle or tool for manifesting your creations. The right form for your product or service can be totally different from what is expected or the norm. Think about your interests that are different from your idea. Practice brainstorming with an open mind.

Look outward, again. Once you have a few format options in mind, look outward to assess the resources you have available or would need to procure for your form options. *What will you need in order to make your idea a reality?* Sometimes starting with a simpler manifestation is realistic in order to start building or developing your product or service. When the idea requires too many resources or it is too expensive, it causes Awake Apprentices to give up. Assess the resources you have and the resources you'll need to make your idea a reality.

Look inward, again. When deciding on the final version of the form to manifest, return to your interests, strengths, and skills. Though a product or service concept sometimes sounds like it will be successful and satisfying, if the process of bringing that concept to reality is not appealing to you, then reconsider the format. Think about if there is a different way to proceed toward the same result that you will enjoy. Make sure to choose a format with a process and a result that is satisfying and fulfills your functionality and inspiration goals.

Sometimes looking outward too much taints our authenticity. We start to copy other people. Copying defeats the whole purpose of creative work and violates the definition of creativity. Spend 20% of your time looking outward and 80% of your time looking inward. Also, remember that your format might change over time. Initially you should stick with a format you choose and see it out. Start from where you are. Then, once you see how that format fulfills your vision, iterate based on the initial product and user feedback.

3. Cultivate the Conditions for Creating

While synthesis can often happen in between working periods when you least expect it, creating is about manifesting and executing, which takes a more dedicated environment. Creativity requires periods of focused time to apply yourself; whether you need to write, build, paint, calculate, or code.

The ideal environment for creativity is one that allows you to focus for sustained periods of time. We don't all have long sustained periods of time in our schedules; however, building some blocks of time into your schedule is necessary whether for 15 minutes, 5 hours, or somewhere in between. **Your progress will be related to how dedicated you are to your creative endeavor and how high you place it on your priority list.** The more time you make for it and the more focus you have, the more progress you will make. You need a non-judgmental atmosphere where you feel you can listen to yourself. *What is an environment that allows you to feel focused and inspired?*

Since the goal is to achieve both functionality and inspiration, it's important to have an environment that fuels productivity and enjoyment. If you work at home, find a place that is quiet and comfortable. If you create in an office space, coffee shop, or other public space, find a location that fuels your focus and your happiness. You can even add elements like flowers or listen to music if that adds value to your creative work environment.

Working from the same environment every day can fuel productivity when working on a project. It's efficient in terms of time. It can also help with consistency of creative thought and technique. However, sometimes it helps to change it up. For some people, working from the same environment for too long can feel stagnant and creativity actually becomes challenging. If you find yourself bored or frustrated with your regular creative environment, change it up! I have a few different environments that fuel my creativity and I work from each depending on how I feel that day and the work I hope to achieve. It takes time to cultivate your perfect environment(s) for creating but once you do, the process becomes more effortless and enjoyable.

While creating, it's also important to set boundaries to eliminate disruptions and distractions. Distractions come from both the physical and digital spaces. It helps to choose a physical space where you will be anonymous, to avoid people stopping by for conversations that take you out of flow. For me, construction sounds are always disruptive so I find a place to do my creative work with minimal surrounding construction work going on.

Though the physical space can offer its fair share of distractions, in our hyper-connected society, the digital space can be even more disruptive. During periods of creativity, turn off your WiFi port if you are doing work on your computer and don't need Internet access. Otherwise, turn off your e-mail and any other distracting apps. Put your phone on silent and place it in a bag or leave it at home or in another room. Notifications and messages are some of the most distracting disruptions that take us completely out of flow. Try to find at least 15 minutes to one hour where you can turn off the tech.

4. Find Your Creative Habits

Your creative habits are your regular rituals and practices that support your creative efforts. Identifying your own creative habits is a process of developing deeper self-awareness and practicing experimentation. Usually, before starting to create something, it helps to have rituals that help you focus and set you up for creative success. Each person has different practices that fuel creativity. **Your creative rituals serve as the structure for your creative process.**

Preparation is essential. Depending on the time of day you choose to create, you might need different practices to transition into the creative process. Many Awake Apprentices are confined by personal or work schedule constraints, and so they must plan creative time according to the time they have. If your creative time is after a busy day at work, a transition activity like yoga or having a cup of tea while reading helps transition your brain into a more calm, focused state. Since I do most of my creative work in the morning, I have a morning routine where I do a short yoga sequence and then make coffee and oatmeal. I sit down, take 10 or so deep breaths. I sit quietly, without distraction, and enjoy my breakfast before beginning to write. Factor this creativity prep time into your creative schedule. **Find an activity or ritual that helps you to transition into a state of deeper focus and aligned action.**

Creative habits also include activities that are inspiring for you. These are practices and techniques that you may not use every day, but they come in handy when you have a creative block or need new inspiration to begin a project. Reading something new, viewing artwork, going to a fitness class, or seeing a movie serve as creative fuel. Find what gives you energy and inspires you along the way. Sometimes doing something tangent to what you think is productive in your creative endeavors can actually get you out of a creative funk and give you new motivation. Creative exercises that I use regularly are mind mapping, walking, free writing, music, and movies. Find the sources of inspiration that fuel your creative process.

Finally, a creative habit is simply to *put aside the time to create*! Especially if you're new to creating, there is never a *good* time to start. It isn't easy to put aside the time, to be alone with your thoughts, or to focus on creating something. Creating usually requires being alone; whether you're alone at your desk, alone in thought and focus, or completely alone without anyone else around. It takes practice to be alone if you're used to being surrounded by others. However, creating is often a solo effort.

Even if your creative project is a team project, your work will likely require solo time. Get comfortable with being alone and embrace it. Once you have your problem to solve or project to work on, put aside the time each day. Maybe, at first, put aside time each week. Get in the practice of creating and it will become easier. Even if you don't make big progress at first, start by putting aside some solo time, thinking about your project, and working on it.

5. Find Talented, Like-Minded Collaborators

Though the foundation for manifesting your creative idea is to put aside the solo time to work, it's also essential to find people to help you manifest your creations. Most Awake Apprentices don't have all of the skills and strengths necessary to manifest their entire idea as a product or service. Most creatives need support, resources, and advice along the way.

Over time, you'll notice where the gaps are in terms of your skill set and capabilities. After some thought about your format and some solo time creating, identify where an expert or a professional could help you to manifest your idea according to your vision. Don't be too shy or proud to ask for help in order to make your idea a reality. Manifesting is a challenge and often requires support from community. **Seek out the right like-minded collaborators to help you bring your vision to reality.** The best collaborators often come from personal references, community groups, or organic meetings.

Also, seek guidance from respected influencers. These are usually people that you respect, who are a bit further along the creative path. Creative advisors can be teachers, friends, family, or formal mentors. Immerse in their creative offerings in order to understand their creative process. You can gain inspiration by taking their class, reading their book, or looking at their website. If you want more support or guidance, ask to meet for coffee to discuss your idea and your roadblocks.

Sometimes opportunities for guidance come in the form of a formal, professional mentorship or coaching period of a few weeks or months. This can be beneficial for overcoming obstacles and staying on track with your creative process. Having someone, whether a friend or a mentor, to offer support and encourage you to stay moving in the direction of manifesting your idea is invaluable.

Strive to learn something new from each person you meet and share your learnings with them. As you'll see in my story, people with complimentary skills and strengths, as well as wise advisors, were essential for my creative process.

My Creativity Story

As I continued to work on my system of exercises for leaders, I felt that my idea was just about ready to take form as a new creative endeavor. I had put my ideas down on paper. I was craving a way to manifest my leadership system as something tangible for others to use and benefit from.

In terms of skills and strengths, I was great at organizing spreadsheets, building number models, and project planning. However, I didn't know where to begin in order to communicate and share my leadership system and exercises. I felt as though I had no creative skills to move this idea from concept to reality. I needed to find a way to manifest this idea in some way aside from just telling people about it over lunch.

I spent time thinking about my skills and strengths. I looked outward and considered how my most respected influencers shared their big ideas as creative endeavors. I realized that the influencers I looked to for practical advice and guidance most regularly shared their work in the form of a book. I love reading but I had no formal writing education or experience. *Could I write a book?* I had never imagined that I, as an engineer, would ever write a book about leadership. However, I was open to the concept. Finally, after some reflection and brainstorming, I envisioned the final product as a guidebook! The book would be organized into seven chapters and each would contain an associated collection of the exercises I had developed.

With this basic form in mind, the vision for the book became clearer each day that I reflected on how to manifest this idea. Even when I wasn't working on it in a dedicated, focused way, ideas would surface. It was also important to spend dedicated time to make progress on the actual product. I used my morning writing time to reflect on the book and to begin writing the content. However, I found that when I sat down to write in the morning, I'd immediately get distracted by work e-mails and the burden of the work day ahead. I realized that I still needed to use my morning writing for work reflection writing to set myself up for the day.

Given my current priorities, I didn't make much progress on the book initially. The time I did spend writing was in short bursts during the day and in longer sessions on the weekends. Even in the times of challenge, I reconnected to my commitment to trust the process and follow my intention. I experimented with different locations on the weekends and found that writing in different coffee shops proved successful. I spent my weekend mornings writing at home, without the normal weekday distractions of work. I spent weekend afternoons at coffee shops. After finding my optimal environments and writing rhythm for each week, I made steady progress on the book. Within a few months, I completed the first draft. It was a very rough first draft but it was a *first* first draft! It felt satisfying.

After the New Year, I started editing the first of many drafts. I also started thinking about how this book would get published. I had moved the idea from concept to paper, but now it needed to go from document to actual book. From my online research and conversation with community at my local bookstore, the publishing process seemed very complex. Getting a publisher seemed like a very remote possibility for many reasons. Luckily, from attending informational events at my local bookstore, I soon learned about self-publishing. Self-publishing would involve a lot more work in some ways - I'd have to design the book, edit the book, proof the book, and figure out my own distribution and marketing. However, I decided that I'd like having control over the content in my final version and control over the process, especially since it was my first time. I set out on the adventure of self-publishing.

I liked self-publishing because I enjoyed having the creative control over my book. I found design software and built each page from scratch. I read a lot online to figure out how to upload my file to the self-publishing platform and order a proof. I was learning a lot through the process! When I received my first proof, I was so amazed and excited. It was a real book! I was so proud of my effort and ability to write and actually create a real book. That spring, I published the book. I told everyone I knew, including my clients and my friends. People were excited for me. However, after a month, to my surprise, the book wasn't selling.

It took me a while to realize that the book, when compared to other professional books, was lacking in a few important areas. When I took the time to step back from my work and really see the book clearly, I realized that the size, font, and interior design were all pretty clunky and amateur. The book was definitely functional but it didn't really look very inspiring or unique. I remember sitting at the coffee shop, flipping through the book and saying to myself, *this could be so much better*. There was a lot of room for improvement. However, I knew that I couldn't do it all on my own. I had my second book in the works already. I needed help in order to really figure this self-publishing thing out. I needed to fill in the skill and knowledge gaps I was missing in order to make this product the best it could be. I wanted it to be **functional and inspiring**.

That summer, I had two books in hand, waiting to be published and re-published. However, I needed some serious design help before I could confidently put these books back out into the world and share them with others. I was fortunate to find two like-minded collaborators to bring my design vision to reality. Working from coffee shops proved to be helpful since I met an artist in my favorite funky coffee shop while mind mapping. We talked, exchanged information, and he re-designed the key graphics for my first book. He transformed my books from technical workbooks to unique creative guidebooks.

I also connected with a wise, experienced book designer through my local bookstore. We had met at a community event where he had presented some of his work and advice for authors. We talked after the event and, when I found myself needing design help, I reached out to him. He was an essential supporter in lifting the quality of the design in terms of the formatting details and the cover. He helped transform my book projects into professional books. **I learned that while we often *can* do it alone, things can be a lot better when we partner with the right creative collaborators.**

It would not have been possible to republish my books without like-minded creative collaborators. After many meetings and conversations, the books were ready to be re-published. It had been almost two years since I had published the first edition of my first book, but all the time and effort was well-worth it. I was finally confident about my final products and satisfied with the quality of the result. The creative process is no easy endeavor. It involves a lot of alone time. However, it is so rewarding to see your idea come to life in a way you could not have imagined. **The creative process is an extension of your potential, beyond the potential you cultivate in the workplace alone. It's an experience of applied learning all its own.** It begins with an idea and a craving to manifest that idea into something that can be seen, shared, and used by other people.

I learned a lot during this process. I learned to cultivate the conditions for my creative process to unfold. I learned that creativity requires freedom and it requires taking a risk. Looking at my books, I see almost all of my experiences – professional and personal – reflected somewhere in the concepts, the words, or the design. All of those experiences of working through challenges, connecting with different kinds of people, completing projects, and travel synthesized and became a brand new book. My creations are a reflection of my Awake Apprentice journey. They are original works. They are creative solutions. The best parts about the process were all of the learnings and connections I made along the way. I learned so much about my own skills and strengths. I learned to reach out for help when I needed it. I have found a way to enjoy both the process and the results of working.

. . .

A year later, my second-edition books started gaining traction. My first book, *Awake Leadership*, was a finalist in a national indie book competition. My second book, *Awake Ethics*, won the grand prize in another national indie book award competition. Going to New York City to accept the prize for *Awake Ethics* was a highlight in my early creative career. I had proven to myself that I could be an author and that, maybe, I could be anything I put my mind to - even something creative. I had not yet become a full-time author, but that wasn't the goal. The goal was to manifest my creative works and forge a new creative, more authentic career.

The path to a more creative career involved a lot work and life changes. My life is like a mosaic; I have pieced together a life and a career that allows me to highlight my strengths and skills that need to shine, to live my days in flow with my needs for possibility, and feel inspired. I am a writer but I am also a yoga teacher, a tutor, and a leadership strategist. I like it this way. It isn't *the* way but it's my way to manifest my creative endeavors and career path. I like the ability to shift gears and give in different ways that highlight my variety of strengths, skills, and interests.

For me, the best part about this kind of creative lifestyle is that you become open to change. I feel more present and able to help in ways that are needed. Making my creative endeavor my purpose and allowing it to lead the way has allowed me to let go of some of my self-centered routines and choices and opt for a more selfless yet free-flowing and authentic lifestyle. **It's not a career path that is planned 20 years in advance but it's a work-life integration approach that allows me to choose vocations that respond to the needs of people and my own needs as well.** The Awake Apprentice path is a path that allows you to reach your own unique potential in your own way.

Creativity

in Action

Creativity Exercises

These six Creativity exercises will help you move from idea to execution. Work through the exercises to turn your idea into a real-world solution or creation!

Exercise 1: From Idea to Mission

Exercise 2: Manifest Your Idea

Exercise 3: Recruit the Right Team

Exercise 4: Your Creative Schedule

Exercise 5: Remember Your Influencers

Exercise 6: Gather Your Inspiration

Supplies:

- Pen or pencil
- Paper
- Journal

Creativity

Exercise 1: From Idea to Mission

Intention*: Get intentional before working on one of your creative ideas.*

What is an idea without sound intention and motivation? Before embarking on your creative journey, you must get intentional about the idea you want to bring to reality. Why is it important? Why do you want to work on it? Why is it worthy of your time and effort, and the time and effort of others? Why is it really needed?

Try this exercise with one of your favorite ideas. If you're not feeling the idea after some reflection and thought, try the exercise with a different idea. Sometimes your favorite idea isn't necessarily the one you should manifest. Go with your intuition and then iterate.

This exercise is a reflection for preparing to take action. Let's go!

in Action

Exercise 1: From Idea to Mission

Of your 20 synthesis ideas, what is the idea you are most excited about working on?

_____

How is this idea functional?

_____

_____

_____

How is it inspiring?

_____

_____

_____

Creativity

Exercise 1: From Idea to Mission

How does this idea align with your interests, skills, and strengths?

_____
_____
_____
_____

What is the intended impact? What is your intention in making this a reality?

_____
_____
_____
_____

in Action

Exercise 2: Manifest Your Idea

Intention: *Take action on your ideas to bring your vision to reality. Execute your creative endeavors to add value to your experience and share your creative contribution with the world.*

In this exercise, you will make the plan for manifesting your idea as a creative project. It's much easier to do the work and follow through when you have a sound plan! If you have made it this far, you have already set the stage for this all-important step. Many people stop at the prompt to come up with original ideas. Even more people walk away from the invaluable opportunity to actually manifest an idea they have. As I talked about in this chapter, many obstacles get in the way of actually taking action on an idea or creative project. However, when you have a clear vision and a plan, it makes it much easier to get started.

The Creative Project Plan is an essential starting point for manifesting your ideas. I often use the phrase, "Plan the work and work the plan." A plan really provides structure for the creative process. In most aspects, creativity is non-linear and so it's easy to get off track or procrastinate executing your idea as an actual project.

You can use this as a starting point for a project at work or your own side project or venture. This plan will serve as your jumping off point for actually bringing your creative vision to reality. You deserve it and the world needs it.

Turn the page to begin!

Creativity

Example of a Creative Project Plan

Idea or Project Name: Awake Ethics

Intention: To help leaders and rising leaders practice more mindful teamwork and collaboration at work.

Objective: To write a book that outlines the 10 ethical principles and practices toward ourselves and others at work.

Manifestation/Format: A book - an interactive guidebook

Learning Goal(s): Learn how to self-publish, learn how to follow-through in writing a book, learn how to design and market.

Value-add(s): Leaders feel better at work and have better results, career growth, team retention, and relationships.

First Step: Draft the introduction and outline the ten chapters.

Time: Complete a draft in 3 months.

Exercise 2: Manifest Your Idea

Each component of the Creative Project Plan provides an essential aspect of structure. However, the simplicity makes it easy to follow and stay focused on what really matters. Below I explain each component of the Creative Project Plan. Use this guidance to build your own on the following page.

Idea or Project Name: Name the idea or creative project.

Intention: What is your intended *impact* on yourself, customers, and the world?

Objective: What is the concrete objective or projected *outcome*?

Manifestation/Format: In what specific *format* will you manifest this idea?

Learning Goal(s): What do you hope to *learn* in the process?

Value-add(s): What specific *value* will this work add to the world?

First Step: What is the first step you need to take to bring this idea to life?

Time: How much time will you put aside each week to work on this project? What day will you start?

Remember that while this project plan is the foundation for your creative project, it's up to you to take action on it!

Creativity

Your Turn!

Idea or Project Name: _____

Intention: _____

Objective: _____

Manifestation/Format: _____

Learning Goal(s): _____

Value-add(s): _____

First Step: _____

Time: _____

in Action

Exercise 3: Recruit Your Team

Intention: *Bring awareness to the outside capabilities, strengths, and expertise you need to make your idea the best it can be.*

Do you have all the skills, strengths, and expertise to manifest your creative idea? It's okay if you don't know right now, but the purpose of this exercise is to help you think about the support you'll need! Impactful creative endeavors are seldom executed completely solo.

In this exercise, you will work through prompts and mind map the support network you'll need. Use your mind map to rank the expertise and skills you'll need to learn and/or recruit from outside professionals.

Creativity

Exercise 3: Recruit Your Team

Based on your skills and strengths, what elements of bringing this idea to life can you start to work on right now?

_____

_____

_____

_____

_____

What skills and strengths - and what type of other professionals - might you need to recruit help from to make your idea a reality?

_____

_____

_____

_____

_____

in Action

Exercise 3: Recruit Your Team

Use the space below to list or mind map the elements of support you'll need. Use color coding to rank the expertise and skills in terms of importance.

Creativity

Exercise 4: Your Creative Schedule

Intention: Design your ideal creative day schedule that will provide new inspiration and energy, and fuel your creative work.

Do your daily rituals, activities, and energy support your creative work? It's important to know what daily elements fuel your positive energy and your creativity. You might not know everything that fuels your best creative work, but this is a place to start. Also, you might know what does *not* fuel your creative work.

For me, the ideal creative day starts with getting enough sleep and waking up with or after sunrise. The day has to be open enough to allow my mind to wander, without too much structure or social planning. I need a quiet space and my creative tools.

In this exercise, you will map the elements that you feel make up your ideal creative daily schedule. Then, you'll organize those elements into a rough daily schedule to kick-off your creative work.

in Action

Exercise 4: Your Creative Schedule

Use the area below to brainstorm the activites and rituals that fuel your creativity. You can list them or make a mind map. *Think: What kind of sleep and wake-up time? What kind of movement? What kind of work timeframe? What kind of food or lunch breaks?*

See my example on the following page for inspiration...

Creativity

Exercise 4: Your Creative Schedule

Example of a activities and rituals mind map and daily schedule:

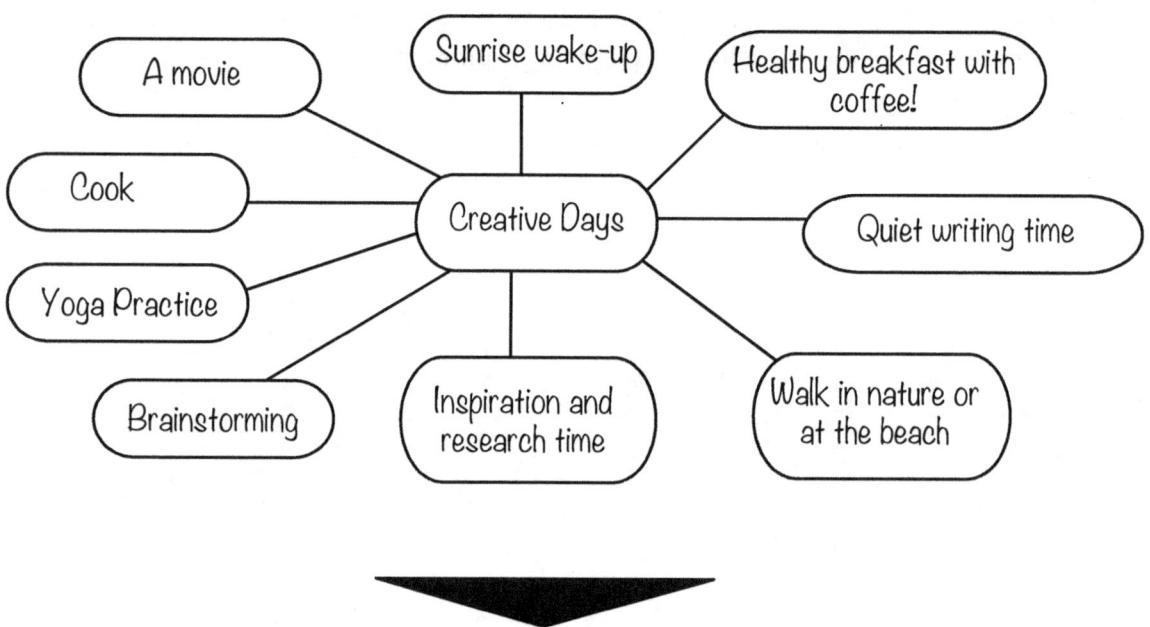

Draft of Creative Day Schedule
7am: Wake-up, stretch, breakfast
7:30 - 11am: Quiet writing time
11am: Walk adventure
12:30: lunch
1:30pm: Research, editing, brainstorming, or writing
4:30pm: Yoga practice
6:30pm: Cook dinner, movie
10pm: Sleep

in Action

Exercise 4: Your Creative Schedule

Your turn!

Draft your ideal creative daily schedule:

Creativity

Exercise 5: Gather Greater Inspiration

Intention: *Expand your sources of inspiration to enhance your creativity and creative work.*

How do you gather new inspiration? Inspiration is the oxygen of creativity. We need new sources of inspiration - new learnings, new perspective, and new motivation to keep creating and to make your unique creations truly functional and inspiring.

So far, most of your inspiration has come from your experiences of relativity. The point of this exercise is to think about things that inspire you, to add new sources of inspiration to your list, and to brainstorm inspiration adventures. This really helps when trying to creatively manifest your idea. You'll need go-to inspirational activities and sources for when you encounter obstacles or a "creative rut".

Sometimes opportunities for inspiration come through activites that you might not perceive as inspiring at first. Work through the map and, optionally, make a vision board to come up with new ways to stay inspired.

Let's go!

in Action

Example of an Inspiration Map:

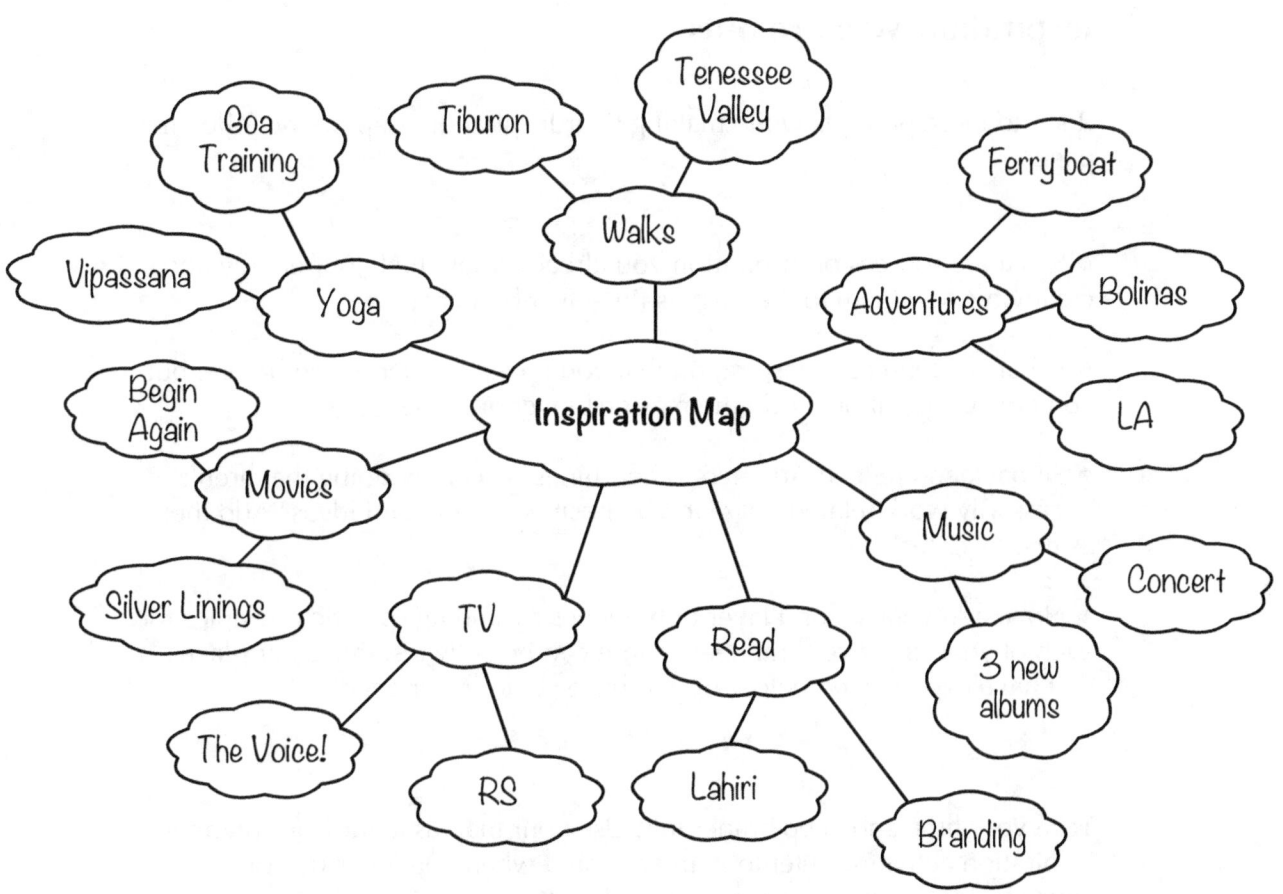

Turn the page to find the prompts and make your own!

Creativity

Exercise 5: Gather Greater Inspiration

Inspiration Map Prompts

Refer to these prompts while making your Inspiration Map on the following page.

• What are sources of inspiration you already know fuel your energy and creativity? Add them to the map as first-layer branches.

• What are sources of inspiration that you haven't experienced before, but you are curious about? Add them as first-layer branches.

• Sit back and reflect: Are there other things you enjoy doing that aren't necessarily work-related but give you positive energy and ideas? Add them as first-layer branches.

• Now, add your second layer of branches by adding specific examples for each of your first-layer branches. These can be activites, things, or places you have experienced before or you have yet to experience.

Take your time and keep branching! Use your map as a guide for planning inspiration activites. Refer to it and act on it when you feel stuck during your creative journey. Continue to add to it!

in Action

Exercise 5: Gather Greater Inspiration

Your turn!

Make your own Inspiration Map:

Creativity

Exercise 6: Help from your Influencers

Intention: Reflect on your key influencers to return to your motivation, generate ideas for manifesting, and refining your style.

For many Awake Apprentices, influencers are such a big part of why they do what they do, and especially why they embark on our on creative endeavors. Your influencers are great people and great role models because you share something in common with them, they offer something that is both functional and inspiring for you, and they do it with grace and style.

Many people agree that we are each a product of the people we hang out with the most. I think this is somewhat true. When I can't decide how to go about something or I encounter an obstacle, I often find myself asking, "How would she do it?" or "How would he respond?".

Your influencers can be leaders (past or present) at work, authors, entrpreneurs, artists, family, friends, or someone else! Work through the prompts to reflect on three of your key influencers to gain fresh inspiration and motivation, and even generate ideas for how to move forward. If you need more space, continue in a separate journal. Look back at this exercise from time-to-time when you need motivation for pushing through creative challenges.

Extension: An extension of this exercise is to write each of your influencers a hypothetical (or real!) letter. Also, you could create a vision board that incorporates your influencers.

in Action

Exercise 6: Help from your Influencers

Influencer 1

Who comes to mind as a primary influencer for you?

_____

Why does this person resonate as an influencer? Is it what they offer, how they do what they do, a key event or act that inspired you?

_____

_____

_____

What is it about who they are and what they do that has changed you as a person? How have they influenced what you want to do in this lifetime?

_____

_____

_____

_____

Creativity

Exercise 6: Help from your Influencers

Influencer 2

Who comes to mind as a primary influencer for you?

_____

Why does this person resonate as an influencer? Is it what they offer, how they do what they do, a key event or act that inspired you?

_____

_____

_____

What is it about who they are and what they do that has changed you as a person? How have they influenced what you want to do in this lifetime?

_____

_____

_____

_____

in Action

Exercise 6: Help from your Influencers

Influencer 3

Who comes to mind as a primary influencer for you?

_____

Why does this person resonate as an influencer? Is it what they offer, how they do what they do, a key event or act that inspired you?

_____

_____

_____

What is it about who they are and what they do that has changed you as a person? How have they influenced what you want to do in this lifetime?

_____

_____

_____

_____

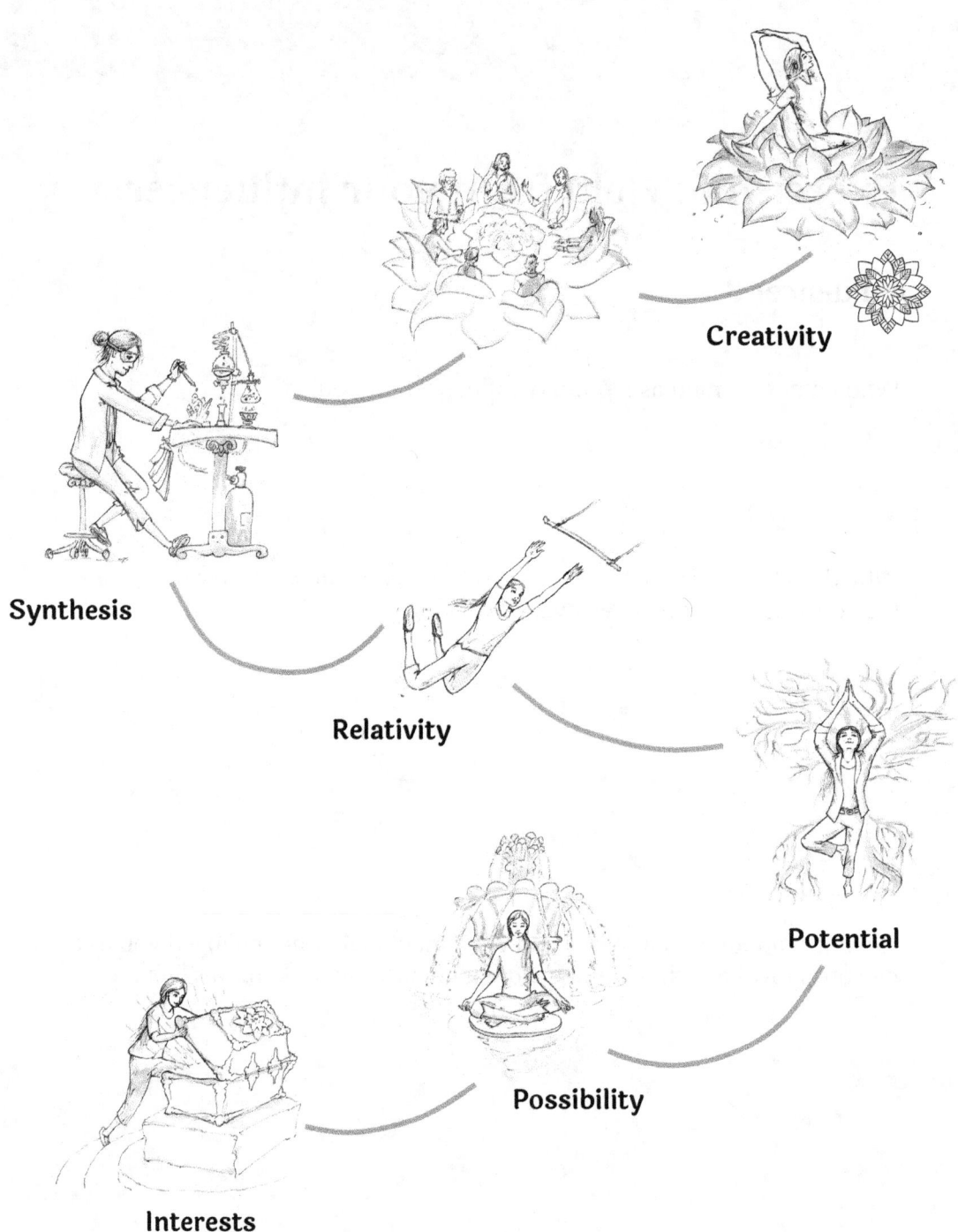

Earth to Creative Leader Tip #6

Go with the Flow

Creative endeavors are best approached with an open mind and a flexible schedule. When creating, Awake Apprentices need a balance of structured and unstructured time. It's hard to be creative when you have a super-structured schedule. Some structure is good, like having a morning routine that works for aligning your body, mind, and spirit in the direction of creating. However, there needs to be a healthy amount of unstructured time in order to stay inspired and keep the creative energy flowing when you catch a wave of productive creative work.

The creative process requires letting go of some type-A tendencies in order to embrace the process and allow creative ideas to surface. **The creative process calls for letting go of the routines and schedules you've been handed, in exchange for looking inward to craft your own schedule and rituals that serve your process.** Allow yourself to experiment with different schedules. Use your draft from exercise 4.

Especially for people used to a structured work and life schedule, the creative process can seem out of control. Change can feel scary at first, but creatives are no stranger to change. You might find that your rituals need to change in favor of new rituals. Instead of going to the gym, long walks in nature may become your new norm. Maybe Wednesday afternoon calls for a matinee movie to refresh. Maybe Thursday morning calls for yoga. Prepare to be weird in order to be productive. Trust the process, experiment with your rituals and schedule, and trust that the process will change periodically.

Conclusions

Conclusions

Congratulations! You have made your way through the path of the Awake Apprentice. I hope you found that the six steps of the Awake Apprentice system serve as a progression toward more understanding and awareness of your unique skills, strengths, and creative potential. In this final section, I'll conclude with a brief review of the Awake Apprentice journey and I'll leave you with three next steps to think about as you continue with your creative vocation development.

Each of the six chapters focused on a different aspect of personal growth and professional development that will enable you to manifest your creations and resolve obstacles along the way. The guidance, stories, and exercises in each chapter show, in action, how to embody the Awake Apprentice system as you navigate your own career. The six steps of the Awake Apprentice system show and tell that you should:

- Lead with your **interests** when searching for a job and when envisioning your career path

- Bring awareness to the conditions of **possibility** that serve your best work and resolve possibility obstacles along the way

- Find a Center of Applied Learning that offers opportunities for **potential** and proactively ask for potential opportunities to learn and grow

- Make transitions with grace and jump into new **relativity** experiences with curiosity and excitement for seeing through new lenses

- Take time and space to practice **synthesis** and reflect on the big questions in order to come up with original ideas, solutions, and creations

- Cultivate the conditions for **creativity** and manifest your vision with intention

The Awake Apprentice System

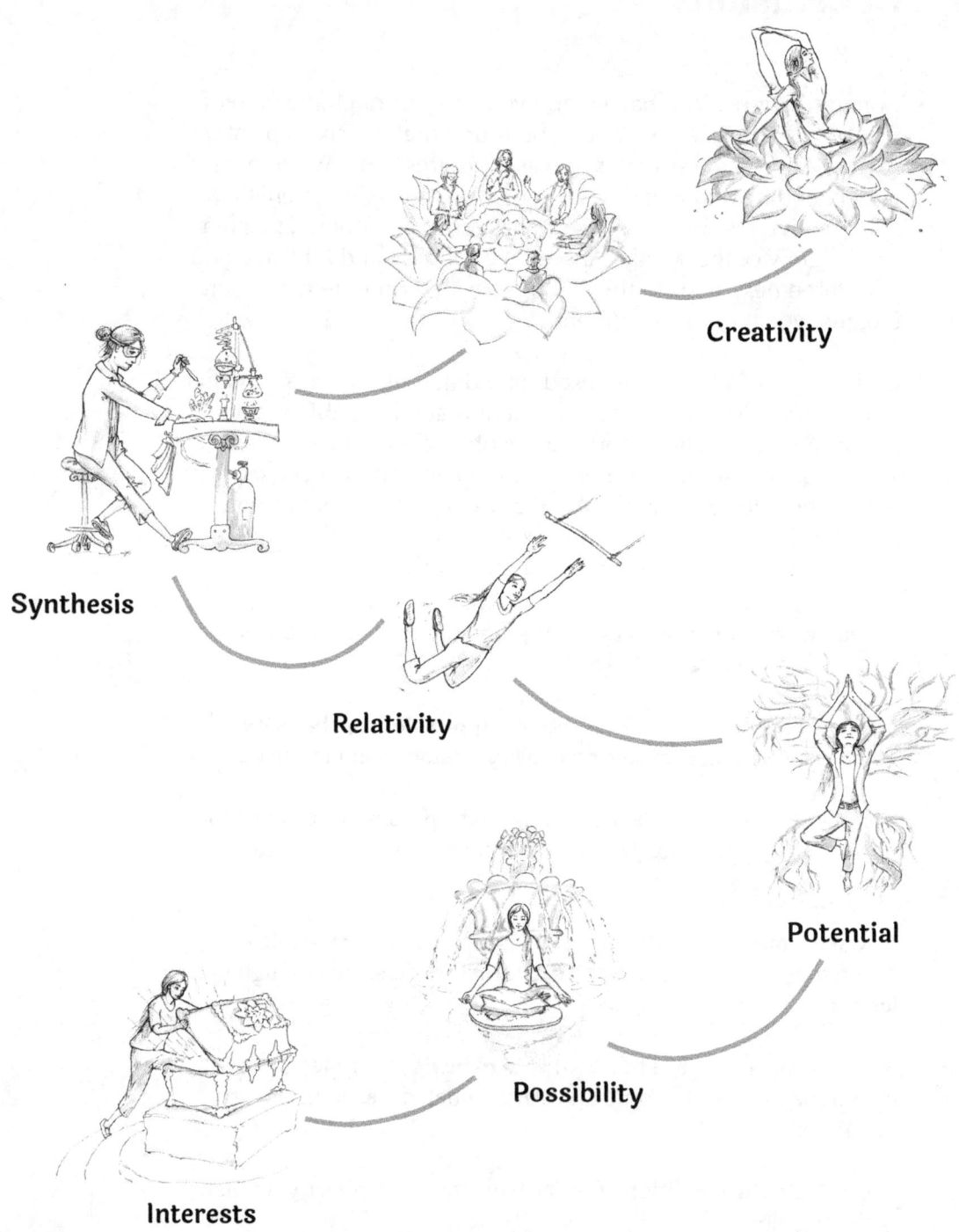

Creativity

Synthesis

Relativity

Potential

Possibility

Interests

Begin here.

By working through this system, I hope that you learned more about yourself and your creative potential. **The Awake Apprentice path is a means for finding work-life integration and healing the common issues we face in modern work and career development.** Continue to use the steps and exercises to find work that has a meaningful impact, that you enjoy, and where you can express your creativity.

While creativity is often subjective and mysterious, my hope is that this system continues to help you begin from where you are to discover (and rediscover) your creativity. The path is not linear, but a series of steps that allows you to start from where you are right now and move toward creativity and more authentic, meaningful offerings in your career.

Creating is both healing and exciting. New creations solve problems and provide inspiration. Before we embarked on the Awake Apprentice path, I mentioned that it is our individual responsibility to lead by example and practice deep awareness, tap into our creative powers, and manifest our creations. To conclude, I'll share three ways to continue to use your creative power for good.

1. Become a Leader of Your Work and Your Life

A leader guides something forward, whether that is an initiative and/or a team. An Awake Apprentice moves his or her career and life forward, and moves humanity forward with new solutions and creations. Therefore, the path of an Awake Apprentice is preparation for becoming a strong leader in work and in life.

By working through the path of the Awake Apprentice, you hone essential skills including courage, self-awareness, empathy, the ability to learn, the ability to problem-solve, and the ability to take action and execute. Whether you realized it or not, as an Awake Apprentice, you are a leader of your work and your life.

Becoming an Awake Apprentice at work also solves the work-life balance crisis. By leading with your interests and tapping into your creativity, work becomes a deeply personal endeavor. This results in work-life integration. True leadership is about embodying what you believe in and represent in this lifetime. **When your work becomes not only a means to an end, but an intentional effort that makes your life, the lives of others, and the world better, you come into full alignment as a leader.**

Leading is the advanced practice of an Awake Apprentice. However, you are all always both an Awake Apprentice and a leader. You should always act as a student of your experience and your team members. You have the ability to guide something forward, develop solutions, and create new things. As you transition from an Awake Apprentice to an Awake Leader, remember that you are always really both - an Awake Apprentice and a leader.

As we saw in the possibility and potential chapters, the path of an Awake Apprentice requires support and guidance from ethical, wise, mentorial leaders. An Awake Apprentice is equipped to become a strong leader because they have been in the shoes of the future Awake Apprentices and this fosters a sense of empathy. We need strong leaders to develop intelligent and enthusiastic Awake Apprentices and future leaders.

To become a strong leader, mentor from your interests and experience. Give your team members possibility, potential, and attention. Lead by example. Give your team experiences of applied learning, where the process and the results are equally as important.

2. Move the Wave of Humanity

Creativity is mysterious, like the wind. The wind starts in a certain direction and makes waves. Waves have ripple effects. As an Awake Apprentice, you not only impact your own career and those around you, but your actions also impact the entire world. By manifesting creations that impact the world in small and large ways, the world changes and moves in a certain direction.

Each creation you contribute and each problem you solve has an impact. The impact is seen in the world after you implement your solution or share your creation. Every solution you implement and every creation you share moves someone, and therefore moves humanity. Creative leaders *move the wave of humanity*. **To create is to make something original that guides the wave of humanity, no matter how small or large the impact is.** It begins at the individual level and expands out to the collective. It's all connected.

During your apprenticeships, you find your creative purpose by following your interests and then, through your own creations, you give it away. You know from experience that your interests help others because they helped you! They help you to feel good, to inspire, and to connect. When you follow your interests, gain experiences, and use your heart to create, you are giving in alignment with what you believe in. You make something originally yours and move the wave of humanity in a positive direction. Your creative power is most likely to stem from something you're interested in and inspired by. Your joy will become the joy of others. Your creations become the interests of the next generation of Awake Apprentices.

The world needs your discernment, your point of view, and your creations to move forward. Most of humanity continues to do things the same way, on autopilot, and collectively follows monopolistic organizations. This is not the approach of an Awake Leader. If we continue to do this, authenticity, health, and creativity will suffer. There is not a one-size-fits all solution for anything. Follow your interests, synthesize your experiences of applied learning, and challenge yourself to design solutions and make new creations. Tap into your limitless creativity and move the wave of humanity in a positive direction.

3. Follow Your Dharma to Build Good Karma

What is *dharma*? Dharma literally means "law". Dharma is a concept from spiritual and yoga philosophy that means calling or purpose. To follow your dharma is to follow your calling and discover your purpose in this lifetime. If you think about it, the path of the Awake Apprentice is really a progression toward discovering your dharma. When we follow our dharma, we find more ease and more meaning. There are always obstacles and challenges along the way; however, when we follow our dharma instead of resisting it, we find more joy, connection, and inspiration every day.

There is another important concept called *karma*, that relates to the path of dharma. Karma is also an ancient concept found in eastern spiritual and religious texts. Karma is a Sanskrit word meaning "action" and in the ancient texts it refers to the cyclical nature of energy. Eventually, you get back what you give. As we can see in the world of commerce especially, but also the world in general, everything is connected.

We have all seen examples of how every action has an impact. Every action has a reaction. We sometimes lose sight of this in our narrow day-to-day activity, but it's true. Your actions, good or bad, small or large, will ultimately have an effect. Your joy will become the joy of others, and their joy will become your joy. **An Awake Apprentice follows their dharma and unique purpose. Therefore, they take intentional action to build good karma.**

Ultimately, this book is a call for Awake Apprentices to follow their dharma – to find their life's purpose by tapping into their creative power. By following your dharma, your unique purpose, you will build good karma. This starts with following your interests rather than what someone told you is helpful, right, or fruitful. It involves doing what you discern is moral and authentic rather than following the status quo.

Your dharma could be to work in an organization that aligns closely with your interests, morals, and lifestyle in order to make the impact or change you want to see in the world. Your dharma could be to travel and teach something close to your heart to other people. Your dharma could be to start your own business in order make a change or impact you wish to see. Your dharma could be to create new original works and share them with the world.

Your dharma is only yours. You are a unique individual with a unique set of skills, interests, and experiences. Only you can follow your dharma and know if you're going in the right direction. The exercises in this book help to foster that sense of direction and intuition.

All of your Awake Apprentice experiences happen for a reason. It's up to you to practice synthesis to harness the learnings, follow your dharma, and create for the next generation of Awake Apprentices. Use your creative powers for good.

As you close this book and start to embody your impact on the world, remember that you are already a leader, you are already moving the wave of humanity, and you are already building karma. This book is a call to do that with awareness and intention in order to move toward your dharma. **You always have the ability to practice awareness and follow your dharma.** You have the strength to become a leader, tap into you creative power, and share your unique creations with others to change the world.

On the following two pages, work through the closing reflection prompts. If you need more space, use a separate journal.

Closing Reflection Prompts

How are you living and working in alignment with your interests? How are you following your interests every day at work and in life?

_____

_____

_____

_____

_____

How will you take the lead in your career and in your creative endeavors? What kind of leader do you aspire to be?

_____

_____

_____

_____

_____

Closing Reflection Prompts

How will you move the wave of humanity in a positive direction with your creations? What is the impact you hope to have on the world?

_____

_____

_____

_____

_____

How are you spreading good karma by following your dharma? What kind of energy are you putting out into the world with your actions?

_____

_____

_____

_____

_____

Appendices

The Pace

A Guide for Working through Awake Apprentice

The sample schedule below gives you some guidance for how to work through the book.

Preface & Introduction	→ Week 1
Chapter 1: Interests	→ Week 2
Chapter 2: Possibility	→ Week 3
Chapter 3: Potential	→ Week 4
Chapter 4: Relativity	→ Week 5
Chapter 5: Synthesis	→ Week 6
Chapter 6: Creativity	→ Week 7
Conclusions	→ Week 8
Reflect, Practice, Observe	→ Week 9

Note: Every Awake Apprentice has their own pace for working through the book. Feel free to move through it at the pace you like. At different times, different sections and exercises will resonate with you.

Recommended Reading

These books will change the way you live and work.

Awake Apprentice was largely inspired by these timeless books.

How Can I Help?
By Ram Dass and Paul Gorman

Eastern Mind, Western Body
By Anodea Judith

The Yoga-Sutra of Patanjali
Translated by Chip Hartranft

The Bhagavad Gita
Translated by Eknath Easwaran

Thank You Notes

Thanks first and foremost to the **Awake Leadership** and **Awake Ethics** readers! Your continued support for the guidebooks and the mission is invaluable.

Thanks to Aaron Bardo for his amazing illustrations that brought the book to life.

Thanks to all the editors and helpers that diligently gave feedback during the writing and design process.

Thanks to my teachers and leaders for sharing your wisdom and giving me experience and opportunities.

About Hilary

Hilary Jane Grosskopf is a leadership strategist, award-winning author, yoga teacher, and entrepreneur. She is a systems engineer by education and discovered yoga during college as a way to find better health and balance at work and in life. She began her early career working in large retail companies in supply chain and transportation. Her writing is inspired by her study of systems, her yoga practice, and her experience as a leader in a variety of organizations. In 2019, she won the Indie Reader Discovery Award in the How-To category for her second leadership guidebook, *Awake Ethics*.

Hilary founded Awake Leadership Solutions in 2017 to help leaders seeking mindful, creative solutions to modern leadership challenges. As Founder of Awake Leadership Solutions, she helps leaders to develop strong leadership skills, build the teams of their dreams, and take command of their career. Her content for leaders has been featured in Leader to Leader magazine, Fast Company, Training Industry, and more.

Learn more about Hilary and Awake Leadership Solutions at
www.AwakeLeadershipSolutions.com

More Books By Hilary

Awake Leadership
A system for leading with clarity and creativity.

Awake Leadership is a system of seven vitals for successful leadership in action. While many leadership books detail qualities of excellent leaders, this guide shows how to lead through a progression of specific practices. Each section of the guidebook contains interactive exercises with examples and tips for putting the vitals into action. Learn practices for aligning and motivating your team. Achieve your collective and individual goals with more enthusiasm and ease.

Available on Amazon.com.

Learn more at awakeleadershipsolutions.com

Awake Ethics
A system for aligning your actions with your core intentions.

Awake Ethics illustrates how a system of ten ethical principles, when put into practice, enable human-centered progress. In order to successfully lead a team or modern organization, leaders must learn how to develop mental resilience and cultivate both peace and progress at work. Through stories from the field, prompts, and interactive exercises, learn how to align your actions with your intentions for connection, creativity, and satisfying progress.

Available on Amazon.com.

Learn more at awakeleadershipsolutions.com

Awake Apprentice

www.ingramcontent.com/pod-product-compliance
Lightning Source LLC
Chambersburg PA
CBHW081105080526
44587CB00021B/3457